It's another Quality Book from CGP

This book is for anyone doing GCSE Resistant Materials.

It contains lots of tricky questions designed
to make you sweat — because that's the only
way you'll get any better.

It's also got the odd daft bit in to try and make
the whole thing at least vaguely entertaining for you.

What CGP is all about

Our sole aim here at CGP is to produce the highest quality
books — carefully written, immaculately presented and
dangerously close to being funny.

Then we work our socks off to get them out to you
— at the cheapest possible prices.

Contents

SECTION ONE — THE DESIGN PROCESS
Design Brief 1
Research 2
Design Specification 3
Generating Proposals 4
Development 5
Evaluation 6
Manufacturer's Specification 7
Planning Production 8

SECTION TWO — TOOLS AND PROCESSES
Hand Tools 9
Machine and Power Tools 10
Deforming 11
Reforming 12
Assembly and Finishing 13
Fabricating — Screws and Bolts 14
Fabricating — Nails, Rivets and Adhesives 15
Fabricating — Joints 16
Fabricating — Joining Metals 17
Computerised Production 18

SECTION THREE — MATERIALS AND COMPONENTS
Properties of Materials 19
Metals 20
Plastics 22
Wood 23
Manufactured Boards 24
Composites and Smart Materials 25
Fixtures and Fittings 26
Adhesives 27

SECTION FOUR — SYSTEMS AND MECHANISMS
Systems 28
Gear Mechanisms 29
Belt Drives, Chains and Pulleys 30
Gears and Belt Drives — Calculations 31
Cams and Cranks 32
Levers and Links 33

SECTION FIVE — MARKET INFLUENCES
Product Analysis 34
Quality Assurance and Control 35
Social Responsibility 36
Consumers 37
The Environment 38
Health and Safety 39

SECTION SIX — INDUSTRIAL AWARENESS
Scale of Production 41
Manufacturing Systems 42
CAD/CAM and CIM in Industry 43
Advertising and Marketing 44
Good Working Practice 45
Jigs, Moulds and Templates 46

Published by Coordination Group Publications Ltd.

Contributors:
Victoria Brereton
Rhonda Dockray
David Found
Chris Gibson
Stephen Guinness
Alan Rix
Alice Shepperson
Claire Thompson
Judith-Ann Wardlaw
Chrissy Williams

With thanks to Alan Nanson for the proofreading.

ISBN: 1-84146-797-9
Groovy website: www.cgpbooks.co.uk

Jolly bits of clipart from CorelDRAW
With thanks to TECHSOFT UK Ltd for permission to use a screenshot from 'DESIGN TOOLS — 2D DESIGN'
Printed by Elanders Hindson, Newcastle upon Tyne

Text, design, layout and original illustrations © Coordination Group Publications Ltd. 2003
All rights reserved.

Section One — The Design Process

Design Brief

Q1 Explain briefly why companies carry out customer research.

Q2 Describe what a design brief is for and what it should include.

Q3 Each of the people or groups of people below have a problem. Write one to two sentences for each one, describing a product that might be able to help.

   a) John has a large collection of CDs in piles on the floor of his bedroom.

   b) Ms Smith's bedroom is relatively tidy except for her dressing table, which is always covered in pots of make up.

   c) The Jones family are constantly forgetting where they put their keys.

Q4 Companies need to be aware of the existing market and existing products when they think about designing and manufacturing a new product. Give three reasons why companies might decide to introduce a new product into the market.

Q5 Explain the following terms in relation to Design and Technology.

   a) identifying a need

   b) gap in the market

   c) consumer research

   c) user group

   d) environment

Hello, Good Evening and Welcome...
Knowing the Design Process is half the battle with D & T. Make sure you know every stage of the process, what it's for, and what order the stages come in. After that, it should be a breeze...

Research

Q1 Research is used to get ideas before you start designing your product. Describe three things that you could aim to find out from your research.

Q2 There are two forms of research — primary and secondary. Primary research is when you collect information yourself and secondary research is when you use information collected by someone else. Say whether each of the sources of information below is primary or secondary.

- a) Internet
- b) questionnaires
- c) letters
- d) books
- e) newspapers
- f) interviews
- g) magazines

Q3 The table below shows three different ways of carrying out primary research. Copy and complete the table using the sentences in the box to say how each one will help you design your own product.

Method of Research	Use
Questionnaires	
Disassembling an existing product	
Measuring an existing product	

> Tells you how a current product is made and how it works. It will help you to decide which materials and processes you need to use and how your product will meet consumers' needs.
>
> Tells you about people's likes and dislikes. This will help you identify market trends and your target group.
>
> Gives you an idea of the weight, size and shape of your product and its sensory features.

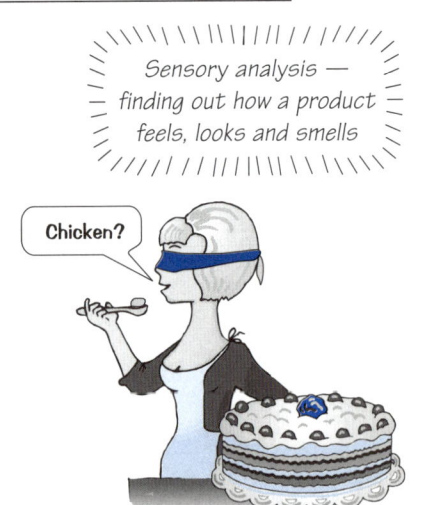

Sensory analysis — finding out how a product feels, looks and smells

"Chicken?"

Q4 Once you have completed your research, you need to decide how to use the information you have gathered. What is the proper term for this stage of the design process?

Section One — The Design Process

Design Specification

Q1 Write a sentence to explain what a design specification is.

Q2 Think of as many factors as you can that could be included in a design specification. Draw a mind map to show your ideas.

Q3 The table below shows the features that should be included in a design specification. Copy and complete the table by matching the terms (in the box) with their meanings.

Term	Meaning
	how long will the product last
	concerns repair when product fails
	the measurements
	the product's job
	what shape, colour, texture etc. will be most suitable

> dimensions   durability   maintenance
> appearance   function

Q4 Below is a list of specification points for different products. Write out the appropriate specification points for each product.

  a) office lamp
  b) cosmetic mirror
  c) disposable lady shaver
  d) computer mouse

> must be ergonomically designed so that it is comfortable to hold and use
>
> designed for a female, must be replaced after use
>
> to be designed so that it is free standing and suitable for a professional environment
>
> designed to be transportable, to fit in a pocket or bag

Q5 Write three points that could be included in the design specification for a CD rack.

Section One — The Design Process

Generating Proposals

Q1 Give a brief description of each of the following terms, and say how they might help you generate ideas for a design proposal.

   a) mood board

   b) brainstorming

   c) an existing product

Q2 Designers use sketches to present their ideas. What is the proper term for labelling and adding notes to sketches?

Q3 Your notes should cover the size and shape of your design. Write down five other things that you could include in your notes in order to explain your ideas.

Q4 There are several different ways of presenting your designs. Choose three different ways, and give a brief description of each one. Write your answers into a table like the one below.

Presentation technique	Description

Mood board — mine's black all over on a Monday morning...

This bit is kind of interesting. The main thing is to get as many different ideas flowing as possible. Then later you can go back and pick out the ones you really like, and forget the ones you don't.

Section One — The Design Process

Development

Q1 In order to develop a design it needs to be explored in detail. Give three features of a design that you could consider during the development stage of the design process.

Q2 It is helpful to produce models when you're developing your design. Give the proper name for a design model and write a sentence to explain why models are useful in the design process.

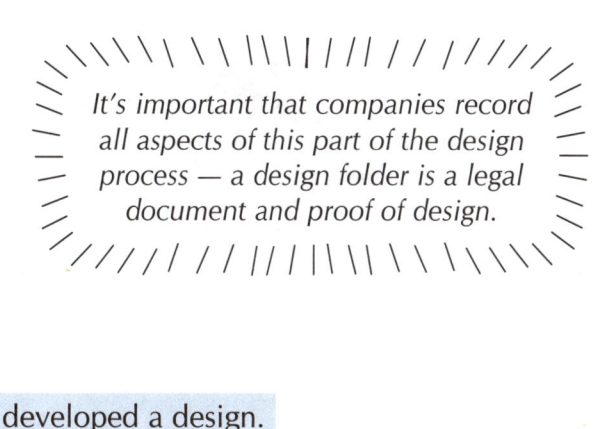

It's important that companies record all aspects of this part of the design process — a design folder is a legal document and proof of design.

Q3 Name three ways you could record how you have developed a design.

Q4 Use the words in the box below to complete the following sentences.

Once you have developed your designs using .... , models or tests, you need to .... the results. This will allow you to make .... to your design and improve the product, or make it ready for .... It is also important that the design is checked to ensure that it meets the ....

> design specification   mass production
> modifications   analyse   sketches

Section One — The Design Process

Evaluation

Q1 Name three ways of testing a product.

Q2 Imagine you have carried out a survey for people to test the product you have designed. Write down five standard questions that could appear in that survey.

Q3 Below are two similar products. Evaluate the two products on the aspects of function, ergonomics and appearance.

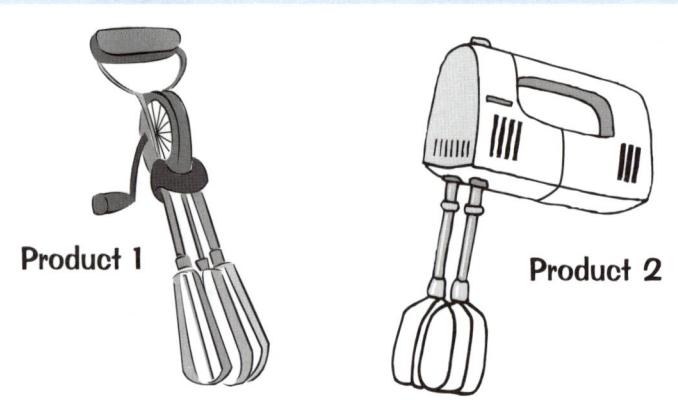

Product 1   Product 2

Q4 Copy and complete the following sentences using the words from the box below.

manufacturing time   assembly process   cost

production   materials   availability

There are a number of things designers need to know once they've finished developing their ideas:

a) The ...., tools and equipment that they will need, and their ....

b) How long it will take to produce each item — the ....

c) How much it will .... to manufacture each item.

d) The .... — the cheapest and most effective way of putting the product together. This will be important when planning for................ .

Section One — The Design Process

Manufacturer's Specification

Q1   What is a manufacturer's specification?

Q2   Manufacturers' specifications are sometimes presented using working drawings. Explain what is meant by working drawings.

Q3   Name one way of presenting a costing sheet on a PC.

Q4   Below is a list of points that should be included in a manufacturer's specification. Copy and complete the sentences using the words from the box.

> tolerances   construction   sizes   finishing
> costs   costings   quality control

a) Clear .... details — explaining exactly how each piece is going to be made.

b) .... — precise measurements of each part.

c) .... — the maximum and minimum sizes of each part.

d) .... details — any special sequencing for finishing.

e) .... instructions — where and how the manufacturing process should be checked.

f) .... — how much each part costs, and details of other .... involved.

Section One — The Design Process

Planning Production

Q1   Explain how charts might help you to plan the production process.

Q2   Describe what a Gantt chart is used for and how it works.

Q3   The graphical symbols below are used in flow charts. Copy them out and use the words on the right to show what stage of a flow chart they represent.

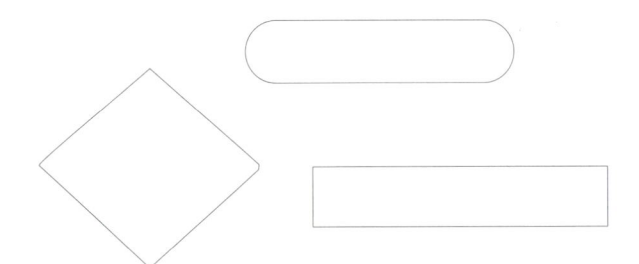

           ◇   (   )   Process

                                Decision

              [   ]   Start / End

Q4   Describe what a summative evaluation is and what it involves.

Q5   Below are seven stages on how to tackle the exam. Draw a flow chart, putting the stages in the right order. Use the correct graphical symbols for each stage.

      Do I have time left (YES or NO) ?   Equipment needed — pen pencil, ruler, rubber, sharpener

    Turn up on time

                     Read through the questions

      TIME UP   Answer the questions

                  Check answers

You can make flow charts for virtually anything...

...like making a cup of tea, for instance. You could even draw some accompanying designs, and annotate them. And while you're drinking your tea, you might like to think about how you're going to hide your designs and what you're going to say if someone asks you what you've been doing for the last two hours.

Section One — The Design Process

Section Two — Tools and Processes

Hand Tools

Q1 Which type of saw is used mainly for cutting curves?

    a) tenon saw   b) ripsaw   c) coping saw   d) hacksaw

Q2 What simple tool would you use to produce a flat, smooth surface on the edge of a piece of mild steel, 6 mm thick?

Q3 Copy and complete the following sentences using words from the box to fill in the spaces.

> gougers   removing material   chisels
> mark out   planes   check

Before .... always .... carefully and then double .... your accuracy. Use suitable tools like bench ...., files, wood ...., drill bits, ... and saws.

Q4 Write down whether the following statements are true or false.

    a) Flat bits are used to make holes for screw heads to sit in.

    b) Cabinet rasps have very coarse teeth.

    c) Hacksaws are used for cutting metals and plastics.

    d) Bench planes are designed to be hit with a mallet.

    e) Gougers are chisels with grooves in them.

Use APPROPRIATE tools

Q5 Copy the table and fill in the gaps.

Tool	Used on which material(s)?
coping saw	a)
cabinet rasp	b)
mortise chisel	c)
fine-cut file	d)
auger bit	e)

Q6 What should you use to chisel a hole in steel sheet?

This stuff couldn't be planer...

Loads of tools to remember here, but you're probably going to be using them all at some point so make sure you learn it all — you'd feel right daft asking for 'that thingemy-jig with twiddly bits'.

Machine and Power Tools

Q1   Write down whether the following statements about machine tools are true or false.

   a)   Machine tools are usually made from thin materials such as polystyrene.

   b)   Machines are usually stationary and bolted to the floor.

   c)   Machine tools are portable and on castors.

   d)   Most machines used for wood are fitted with dust extraction.

   e)   A circular saw has a blade in a long, flexible loop.

Q2   Explain briefly what lathes are mainly used for.

Q3   What is a sanding disc used for?

Q4   The picture shows a tool used to shape metals and sharpen hardened steels. What is it called?

Q5   Name a machine that can be used to create accurate flat surfaces.

Q6   The tool in the picture is a jigsaw. It can make straight or curved cuts in various materials. Describe two features of the machine that enables it to do the work.

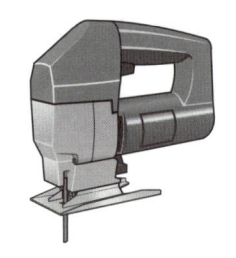

Q7   Copy and complete the following sentences, using some of the words from the box to fill in the spaces.

| shavings of wood | faster | rough shaping |
| less effort | more accurate | power planer |

   A .... is used to remove .... It can be used for a smooth finish or for ....

   It has the advantage that it is .... than a bench plane and needs ....

Section Two — Tools and Processes

Deforming

Q1 Explain the term 'deforming' in the context of shaping woods and metals.

Q2 Say which of the following would be the best to use when making a curved wooden rocking chair runner.

   a) blow moulding   b) laminating
   c) vacuum forming   d) strip heating

Mum... Flopsie's been playing on the deformer again.

Q3 A video recorder casing is made from thin steel. It could be hand made by various methods. Name a process that would be suitable for the small batch production of such a casing.

Q4 A door knocker has been forged by a craftsman. Briefly describe the process, naming the tools that would be used.

Q5 A photograph frame is made by bending an acrylic sheet to shape. Briefly describe a suitable process for bending the acrylic.

Q6 Electric plugs are usually made from thermosetting plastic. Name a suitable process for doing this.

Q7 Use annotated drawings to show the three main stages in the blow moulding process.

Q8 Draw a suitable mould that would make a hemispherical domed lampshade in acrylic.

Q9 Which of the following are needed for press moulding?

   former   mould   air jet   coil
   clamp   high temperature   pressure   plastic powder

Section Two — Tools and Processes

Reforming

Q1 Use two sentences to describe precisely the process of die casting.

Q2 Draw up a simple flow chart to explain the process of injection moulding.

INJECTION MOULDING

plastic granules

heater

PRESSURE

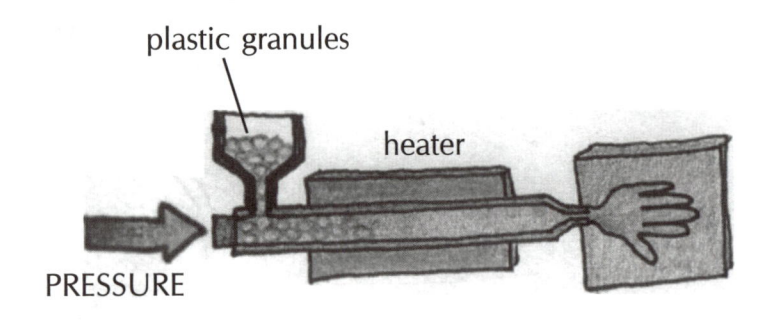

Q3 Name two advantages that injection moulding and extrusion have in common.

Q4 Explain the process of extrusion with a single annotated drawing.

Q5 Name a process that could be used to mould a set of chess pieces at home.

Q6 Which method would you use to mass-produce plastic-covered electric wiring?

Mouldfinger — the new Bond film out soon...
With reforming, the metal or plastic is first melted and then shaped in some way. It's easy to remember the main reforming processes using DIE — Die casting, Injection moulding and Extrusion.

Section Two — Tools and Processes

Assembly and Finishing

Q1 You have made all the parts for a jewellery box. Write out the statements for the sequence of assembly and finishing operations in the <u>best order</u>.

   a) put glue in joints
   b) sand inside surface
   c) fit hinges
   d) cut box into two parts
   e) clamp box together
   f) varnish outside surfaces
   g) fit top and bottom
   h) line inside with fabric
   i) sand outside surfaces

Q2 What is a good sequence of actions for painting a child's toy that is currently bare wood? Copy out the following statements in the best order.

   paint with undercoat and rub down when dry   clean up with glass paper
   paint with gloss coat   paint with primer and rub down when dry

Q3 Materials need to be protected from the weather. De-greaser, etching primer, undercoat and cellulose paint are all used on what material?

Q4 When assembling a cabinet, what does the term 'a dry run' mean?

Q5 Name two different ways of holding wooden pieces together while the glue dries.

Q6 Copy out the sentence and fill in all the gaps.

   touched   cleaned   clean   stop
       greasy   gluing   joints   soldering

If the .... of the final product are to be held together by .... , ... , brazing or welding, it is important to make sure that all the joint areas are ....

The joints must not be .... after they have been .... because .... fingerprints can .... the joint from working.

Section Two — Tools and Processes

Fabricating — Screws and Bolts

Q1 In your own words explain the term 'fabricating'.

Q2 Describe the differences between a machine screw and a bolt.

Q3 In the table are various facts concerning fasteners. Rewrite the table below, matching up the fasteners on the left with the facts on the right.

Fastener	Fact
self-tapping screws	are plated with zinc, brass or chrome
screws and bolts	require pilot and clearance holes
woodscrews	have hardened threads

Q4 Threading is done with tools called taps and dies. Draw these tools in a clear style.

Q5 There are female threads and male threads. What are the differences between them?

Q6 Copy and complete the following sentences.

> self-tapping   tap   bolts   male thread   spanners   split die   machine screws

a) A round rod can be made to fit a threaded hole by cutting a .... onto the rod.

b) Bolts are tightened with ....

c) A .... is used to cut a female thread.

d) .... and .... are used with washers and nuts.

e) .... screws are designed to cut their own threaded holes.

f) A .... is used to cut a male thread.

Q7 Draw a diagram of a bolt and label the following parts.

a) head

b) shank

c) thread

Section Two — Tools and Processes

Fabricating — Nails, Rivets and Adhesives

Q1 A wooden box is to be made with a thin plywood top and bottom.

    a) Describe in a logical order how you would best permanently fasten the top and bottom to the sides.

    b) How should you finish the surfaces prior to painting?

Q2 These pictures show the pop riveting process. Briefly describe how it works.

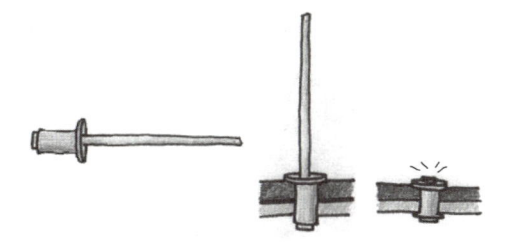

Q3 Name an adhesive that could be used when joining:

    a) wood to wood   b) wood to metal

Q4 Fabrication is often a trade-off between speed and strength. Describe one joining method that is quick but not strong and another that is strong but not quick.

Q5 Sometimes you can only have access to the work from one side of it. Name three totally different types of fasteners that can be used from only one side of the workpiece.

Q6 Copy and complete the following sentences.

> wood   nail punch   hammer-like   reinforce
> riveting   pop   adhesive   sheet metal

    a) A set is a .... tool used for ....

    b) Epoxy resin is a type of ....

    c) Nails are only used in ....

    d) The head of a nail can be hidden below the surface using a ....

    e) Adhesives are often used to .... other methods of fabrication.

    f) .... rivets are a quick and easy method of joining ....

Nail this stuff — stick it in your brain...

Remember all the different ways of joining materials together and when it's best to use each one — always think about the most suitable method for the product you're making.

Section Two — Tools and Processes

Fabricating — Joints

Q1   The pictures show eight joints for joining wood together.
Copy the diagrams of the joints and label the names on them.

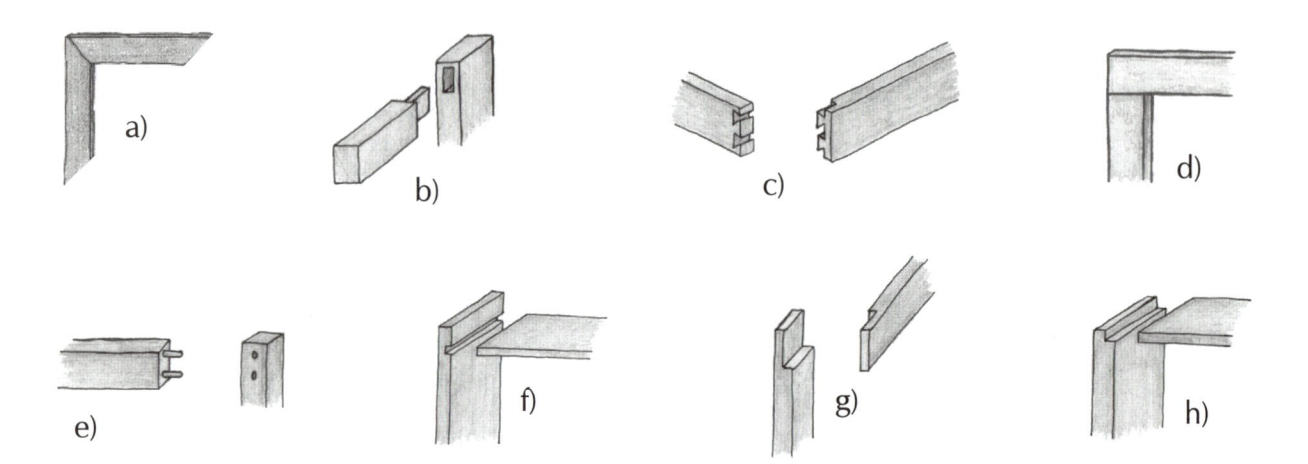

Q2   When joining wooden boards together, why is it better to cut joints instead of just gluing them directly?

Q3   Some joining methods are non-permanent but are still called joints. What is the general name for these joining methods?

Q4   Place the following types of join in order of strength (weakest first).

   a)   glued dovetail joint

   b)   glued butt joint

   c)   knock-down joint

Q5   Copy and complete the table about common uses of different sorts of joint.

Joint	Example of Use
dovetail	
	picture frames
	tables and chairs
butt	
knock-down fittings	
housing	

Section Two — Tools and Processes

Fabricating — Joining Metals

Q1 Metals can be joined permanently using heat. Name three of these processes.

Q2 When a heat process is used to join metals the joint needs to be carefully prepared. Describe, in the form of instructions, the brazing process (including preparation).

Q3 The drawing shows some electrical components that need to be joined permanently. What is the name of the process used?

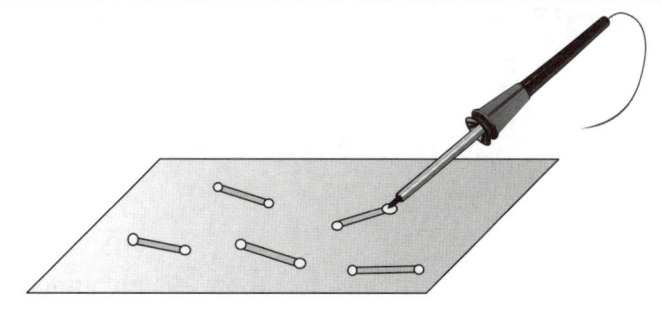

Q4 In your own words, explain the benefit of using a flux when joining metals together.

Q5 Copy the following statements and say whether they are true or false.

   a)   A blow torch can be used for brazing.

   b)   Soldering is a very high temperature process.

   c)   Flux is used for soldering, brazing and welding.

   d)   Brazing is the strongest method of joining metal.

   e)   A soldering iron is used for welding.

   f)   Solder is made of tin and lead.

   g)   A protective face mask is needed for welding.

   h)   Flux allows the surface of the join to oxidise when it's heated.

Section Two — Tools and Processes

Computerised Production

Q1 The use of computers as design tools is now widespread.
Why are they so useful for the business of designing?

Q2 The picture shows a simple example from a simple CAD software package.
Write a list of three advantages of using this software.

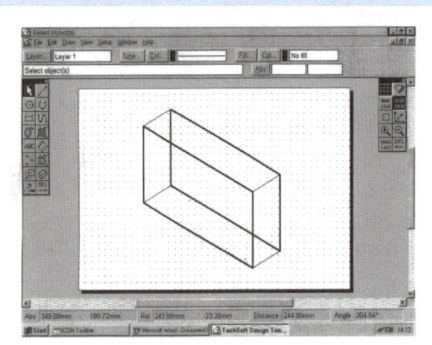

Q3 In your own words, explain the meaning of the term 'computer numerically controlled'.

Q4 Copy the table below and list three advantages and three disadvantages of using CNC machines.

Advantages	Disadvantages

Q5 Designers need to share their work with the people who make the product.
How can CAD help the designer to help the production team?

Q6 Copy and complete the following sentences.

> Computer-Aided Manufacture   data   computer
> tool head   Computer Numerically Controlled

CAD can be used to send information to machines on a production line. This is called .... CAM machines are .... and have onboard .... processors that interpret the CAD .... and control the movement of the ....

Section Two — Tools and Processes

Section Three — Materials and Components

Properties of Materials

Q1 A material's strength is a measure of its ability to withstand forces without breaking. Copy and complete the following sentences by choosing the right form of strength from the box below.

1) If a material has .... strength, it can withstand pulling forces without breaking.

2) If a material has .... strength, it can withstand squashing forces without breaking.

3) If a material has .... strength, it withstands forces trying to bend without breaking.

4) If a material has .... strength, it withstands strong sliding forces without breaking.

5) If a material has .... strength, it can withstand twisting forces without breaking.

| shear | compressive | bending | tensile | torsional |

Q2 Materials can be grouped according to their "hardness". Describe what is meant by the term "hardness".

Q3 What term is used to describe a material that can change its shape, without it cracking or breaking?

Q4 Describe how a material will behave if it is "brittle".

Q5 What is the opposite of brittle?

Q6 What term is used to describe a meterial that is resistant to wear and tear, weathering and corrosive attack?

Q7 Copy and complete the table below by giving an example product for each of the properties listed. The first one has been done for you.

Property	Example Product
hardness	drills and files
plasticity	
brittleness	
toughness	
durability	

Section Three — Materials and Components

Metals

Q1 Metals can be classified into two groups — ferrous and non-ferrous metals. Say whether each of the following points refer to ferrous or non-ferrous metals.

a) Metals that contain iron.

b) Metals that don't contain iron.

c) Metals that are usually magnetic.

d) Metals that don't rust.

Q2 Copy and complete the following table about three common ferrous metals:

Ferrous Metal	Properties	Example Uses
Mild Steel		nuts and bolts
High-Carbon Steel		
Stainless Steel		

Q3 Copy and complete the following table about three common non-ferrous metals:

Non-Ferrous Metal	Properties	Example uses
Aluminium		
Brass	malleable, ductile and attractive	
Copper		pipes

Q4 Describe what an alloy is, and what advantages it may have over a pure metal.

Q5 Say whether each of the following sentences is true or false.

a) Mild steel is an example of a non-ferrous metal. It can be used to make nuts and bolts.

b) Aluminium is an example of a ferrous metal. It is often used to make drinks cans.

c) Ferrous metals contain iron and are usually magnetic.

d) Metals are only available in a small range of shapes and sizes.

e) Alloys can be grouped as ferrous and non-ferrous.

Section Three — Materials and Components

Metals

Q1 <u>Annealing</u>, <u>hardening</u> and <u>tempering</u> are three different types of heat treatment used for changing a metal's properties and characteristics. Describe briefly what each process involves.

Q2 When steel is <u>tempered</u> it will change colour. This indicates how tough it has become. Copy and complete the diagram below, filling in the appropriate colours.

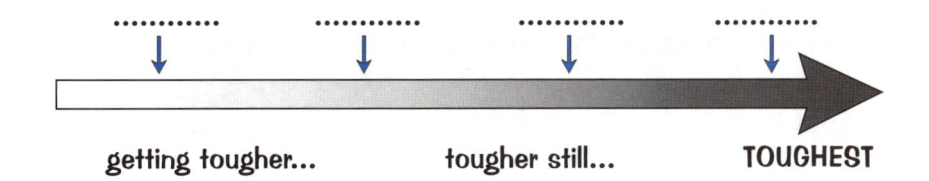

....

getting tougher...   tougher still...   **TOUGHEST**

Q3 When preparing and painting a metal, there are three different stages you need to go through. Name and briefly describe each one.

Q4 In your own words, describe the process of plastic coating.

Q5 Copy and complete this sentence about polishing. Use the words in the box to fill the blanks.

Polishing can be carried out by .... or by using a ....,

which is coated with an abrasive .... The metal is then polished

until the required .... is achieved.

| buffing wheel | hand | polish | surface finish |

Q6 <u>Lacquering</u> means applying a thin layer of cellulose, gum or varnish, which leaves a transparent coating. Describe why this is done and give an example of an item you might do this to.

Varnishing is hard work — in fact, it's lacquering...

If you're struggling to remember all these different examples — don't worry. The basic facts you should try to remember are the three different categories of metal, along with one or two examples of each one. Just don't go writing about Slipknot — examiners don't laugh.

Section Three — Materials and Components

Plastics

Q1   There are two catagories of plastic — thermoplastics and thermosetting plastics. Describe three of the main differences between them.

Q2   Copy and complete the table below by sorting the different plastics into the appropriate columns.

Thermoplastics	Thermosetting Plastics

epoxy resin   acrylic   ABS   polyester resin   polystyrene
polythene   melamine-formaldehyde   urea-formaldehyde

Q3   Pre-processed plastics (for processing into finished products) and processed plastics both come in several different forms. Write down three different forms of each sort of plastic.

Q4   Write a sentence to explain why plastics don't need protective surface finishes to be applied.

Q5   Describe one way to improve a plastic's appearance and get rid of scratches.

Q6   Plastizote is one of several new plastics that have recently been developed. Say what plastizote is, and explain what's so great about it.

Section Three — Materials and Components

Wood

Q1   Copy and complete this summary table about softwood.

Definition of Softwoods	
Rate of Growth	
Cost (in relation to Hardwoods)	
Three Examples	

Q2   Copy and complete this summary table about hardwood.

Definition of Hardwoods	
Rate of Growth	
Cost (in relation to Softwoods)	
Three Examples	

Q3   The following sentences describe different sorts of finish for wood. Match each sentence with the finish it's describing.

1. It's available in a range of colours but is often clear. It's used to seal and protect the surface of the wood, giving a smooth finish.

2. This finish is used to maintain the natural appearance of the wood, and offer extra protection.

3. This finish is used for its colour. It's water-based, so it won't protect the wood from water.

4. This will enhance the appearance of the wood's grain, but will not usually provide extra protection for the wood.

5. A more expensive finish, giving a tough, waterproof finish.

    a)   Woodstain
    b)   Polyurethane Varnish
    c)   Oil
    d)   Polyurethane Paint
    e)   Emulsion Paint

Section Three — Materials and Components

Manufactured Boards

Q1 Name each of the five sorts of manufactured boards pictured below.

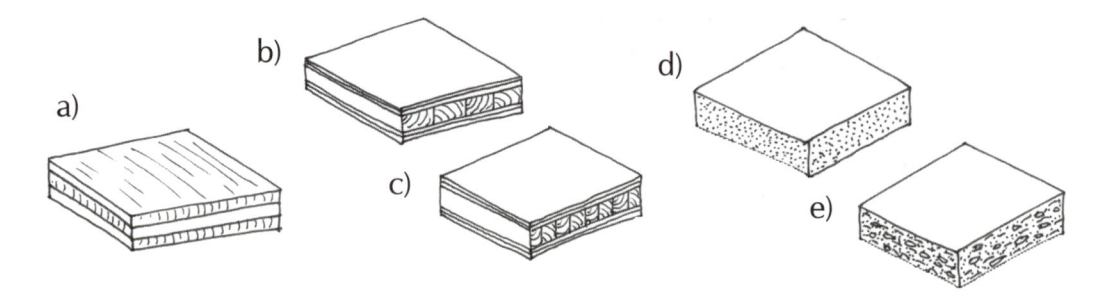

a)   b)   c)   d)   e)

Q2 Describe three advantages that most manufactured boards have over solid woods.

Q3 Why are the different layers within plywood glued together with their grain at 90° to each other?

Q4 Look at the following plywood examples below. Which one are you unlikely to be able to buy, and why?

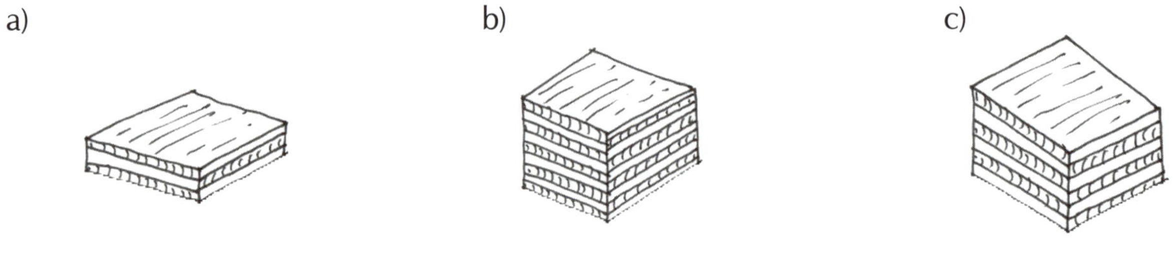

a)   b)   c)

Q5 Describe what blockboard and laminboard are made up of, and how they are different from each other.

Q6 What do the initials MDF stand for?

Q7 Chipboard is not very strong. Write a sentence to explain how it's constructed, and another to say how it is sometimes made stronger.

Pining for the fjords? — this parrot's not pining, it's passed on...

Manufactured board is pretty cool. It's well cheap and you can get it in enormous sizes, but if you ask me you can't beat a nice bit of solid wood for quality and appearance. Ahhhhhhh... wood. REAL wood. Nice bit of Scots pine. Or maybe the larch.

Section Three — Materials and Components

Composites and Smart Materials

Q1 What is a "composite material"?

Q2 Write a sentence describing the benefit of forming composite materials.

Q3 Here are three examples of composite materials. Describe what they are made from and give one example of what each is used for.
   a) Tufnol
   b) Glass Reinforced Plastic (GRP)
   c) Carbon Fibre

Q4 Shape memory alloy is an example of a smart material. Give the name of an example of a shape memory alloy and describe what clever properties it has.

Q5 Name one common use of silicon.
                (in industry)

Q6 Copy and complete these sentences using words from the box below.

Silicon is a .... This means that its resistance .... as its temperature ....

Single .... of silicon are cut into thin wafers and have .... etched onto the surface.

A large chip of 20 cm .... can contain up to one thousand million circuit ....

crystals	semiconductor	elements
increases	decreases	transistors	diameter

see no silicon   hear no silicon   eat no silicon

Section Three — Materials and Components

Fixtures and Fittings

Q1   Here are some sketches of four basic types of hinge.
     Copy the sketches, then name and briefly describe each hinge.

   a)   b)   c)   d)

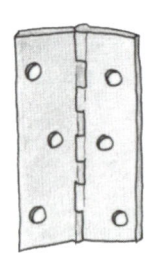

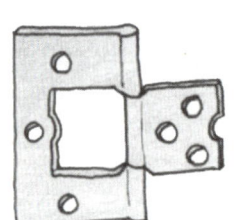

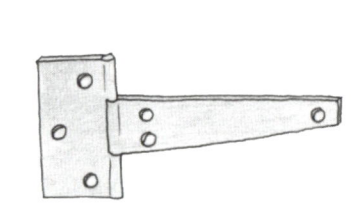

Q2   Say whether the following statements are true or false.

   a) The part of a hinge that moves is called the knuckle.

   b) Hinges are always made of steel because it is strong.

   c) Hinges can be coated in brass, or chrome or enamel in order
      to match a piece of furniture or give a protective finish.

   d) It doesn't really matter which hinge you choose for a
      particular job as any hinge would probably fit.

Q3   When making a cupboard with a door, there are a number of
     different fittings which would help to keep the door shut.
     Name the two main types, and give a brief description of each one.

Q4   Most fixtures and fittings are made from either steel, plated steel or brass.
     Why are these materials suitable for this purpose?

Q5   Fittings are available for holding shelves in position (e.g. inside a kitchen cupboard
     or a bookcase). What advantages do these have over cutting a housing joint?

Q6   Leg fastenings are available to replace the more traditional mortise and
     tenon joint. Write a sentence for each option, to explain it's advantages.

I butt you were expecting some kind of toilet humour...

Choosing the right hinge for a door, gate or whatever can make a huge difference to how well it works. Sometimes the subtle things make a difference, you know. Like if you buy a skirt and it's got velcro fastening at the waist instead of a button so you snag your poshest tights on it...

Section Three — Materials and Components

Adhesives

Q1 What does PVA stand for?

Q2 There are two different types of PVA used for wood working — interior and exterior. What's the difference between them?

WARNING: PVA and shampoo may look alike, but they are NOT interchangeable.

Q3 Copy and complete this sentence using one of the endings below:
The right way to apply contact adhesive is to...

   a)   ...apply glue to both surfaces and stick the pieces together immediately.

   b)   ...apply the glue to both surfaces and wait about 10 minutes until the surfaces are tacky. Then bring the surfaces together and they will be stuck instantly.

   c)   ...spread on the glue and then apply constant pressure for 30 minutes until it is fully dry.

Q4 Which type of glue is Araldite the trade name for?

Q5 Give an example of one or more materials that Araldite can be used to stick together. Briefly describe the main advantages of using Araldite.

Q6 Why is it rather important that you are careful when using superglue?

Q7 What type of glue is used for sticking plastics together?

Learn everything about glue — go on, get stuck in...

All you need to know are the five different types of glue and what each is used for. Make life easier by remembering CAPES — Contact adhesive, Acrylic cement, PVA, Epoxy resin and Superglue.

Section Three — Materials and Components

Systems

Q1 A system has various parts that work together to perform a set function. Copy and complete the following diagram, including the names of the three elements all systems can be broken down into.

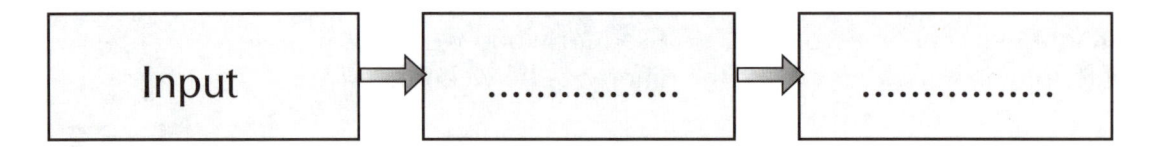

Input → .... → ....

Q2 An example of a system is a bicycle. Describe what the input, process and output are.

Q3 A bicycle can be broken down into a number of smaller subsystems. Name three of these subsystems and say which part of the bike make them up.

Q4 Mechanical systems are often designed to make a particular job easier to do. What name is used to describe this concept? Give an example to help explain this idea.

Q5 Copy and complete the following descriptions, by matching them up with the right type of motion.

a) .... is where something is moving in a straight line.

b) .... is circular movement.

c) .... is where something is moving backwards and forwards in an arc.

d) .... is movement backwards and forwards along a straight line.

> oscillating motion   linear motion
> rotary motion   reciprocating motion

No more linear motion for YOU little johnny...

With a system you can make even the most interesting things dull...

It seems a bit weird forcing every system into the same shaped hole, but as a designer it makes things a lot easier if you think of it this way. And I'd know all about that of course because I'm such a famous designer, oh yes...

Section Four — Systems and Mechanisms

Gear Mechanisms

Q1   Gears are toothed wheels which interlock together, transmitting motion.
     In a simple gear train of two gears, the gears are given different names.
     What are the names given to the two gears? Explain the difference between them.

Q2   In the following gear train examples, if the **driver gear** is always turning clockwise, then write down which direction the **last driven gear** is turning in each case.

   a)

   b)

   c)

   d)

Q3   If the gears within a gear train are different sizes they will turn at different speeds.
     Write down the name of the relationship between the number of teeth on each gear.

Q4   Copy and complete the following descriptions of some different types of gears.
     Write the gear names from the box into the appropriate description.

   a)   .... are used to turn rotary motion into linear motion.

   b)   .... change the direction of rotation through 90° — the gears fit together at right angles.

   c)   .... are where more than one gear is fixed to the same shaft.

   d)   .... change the direction of rotation through 90° and greatly reduce the speed of the movement.

worm gears	rack and pinion gears
bevel gears	compound gears

Q5   Make simple sketches of the four different gear types described in the last question.

Section Four — Systems and Mechanisms

Belt Drives, Chains and Pulleys

Q1 A pillar drill is a good example of a belt drive mechanism. Match labels A, B and C with the words below.

   drill shaft

   flexible belt drive

   motor shaft

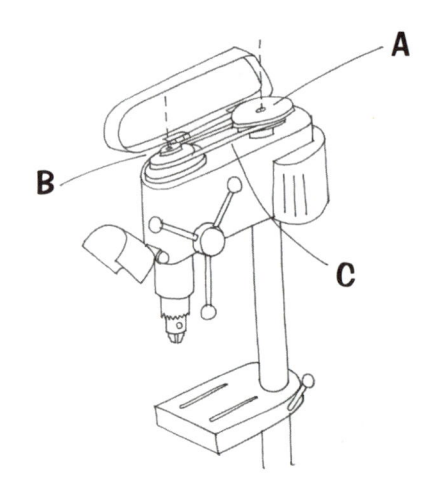

Q2 Give an example of a chain and sprocket mechanism, and describe how it works.

Q3 What is the main advantage of a chain and sprocket mechanism over a belt drive?

Q4 Write out the formula required for calculating the speed of the pulleys within a belt drive mechanism.

Q5 The belt drive system below has been taken out of a pillar drill.

   a) Which position does the flexible belt need to be in to make it go the fastest?

   b) Which position will make it go the slowest?

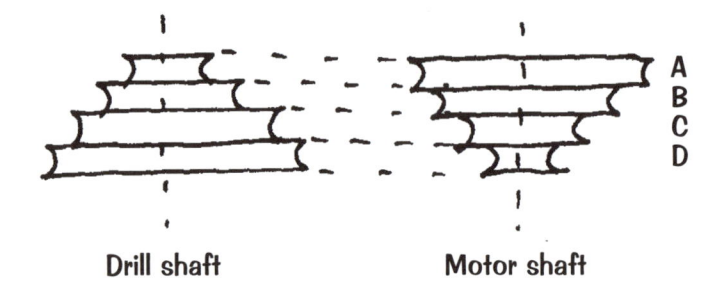

   Drill shaft   Motor shaft

Q6 Say whether each of the following statements are true or false.

   a) Pulleys are one way to gain mechanical advantage.

   b) A single pulley will make a load lighter.

   c) A single pulley will reverse the direction of a force.

   d) Using a block and tackle system will make a heavy load easier to lift.

Section Four — Systems and Mechanisms

Gears and Belt Drives — Calculations

Q1 For the following gear trains, work out how many times the driven gear will turn if the driver gear makes one complete rotation.

a) Driver Teeth = 10, Driven Teeth = 20

b) Driver Teeth = 20, Driven Teeth = 10

c) Driver Teeth = 5, Driven Teeth = 15

d) Driver Teeth = 10, Driven Teeth = 10

e) Driver Teeth = 28, Driven Teeth = 7

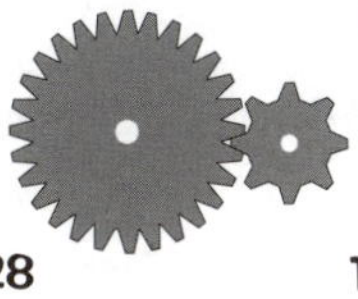

Q2 Using the given formula calculate the RPM (revolutions per minute) of the driven pulley in the following belt drives.

RPM of the driven pulley = $\dfrac{\text{RPM of the driver pulley} \times \text{diameter of the driver pulley}}{\text{diameter of the driven pulley}}$

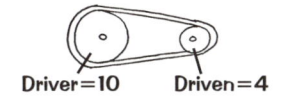

Driver=10, Driven=4
a) driver diameter = 10cm and RPM = 100
driven diameter = 4cm and RPM = ...

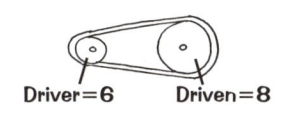

Driver=6, Driven=8
b) driver diameter = 6cm and RPM = 100
driven diameter = 8cm and RPM = ...

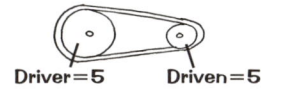

Driver=5, Driven=5
c) driver diameter = 5cm and RPM = 100
driven diameter = 5cm and RPM = ...

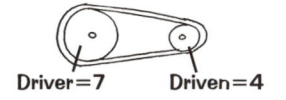

Driver=7, Driven=4
d) driver diameter = 7cm and RPM = 100
driven diameter = 4cm and RPM = ...

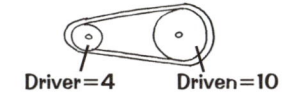

Driver=4, Driven=10
e) driver diameter = 4cm and RPM = 100
driven diameter = 10cm and RPM = ...

My driver has 7 teeth — I call him grandad...

This page gives you some examples of the type of calculation you might need to do in the exam, as part of a mechanisms question. Make sure you understand how to use the formulas. Go on then...

Section Four — Systems and Mechanisms

Cams and Cranks

Q1 Copy and complete the following sentence, by inserting the missing words from the box.

A cam and .... convert .... motion into .... motion.

> *rotary   follower   reciprocating*

Q2 Say if each of the following statements are true or false.

 a) A cam mechanism has two main parts — the cam itself and the follower.

 b) The cam is a rotating shape and is always round.

 c) The cam usually moves up and down, while the follower goes round and round.

 d) All cams can only be rotated in one direction.

Q3 Sketch the following cams and describe the motion of the follower for each.

 a) circular cam (offset)

 b) snail cam

 c) pear cam

 d) four-lobed cam

Q4 Which two cam shapes can only turn in one direction? Explain why.

Q5 A simple crank is a handle on a shaft. In order to get this old car started, which crank handle would be the easiest to turn, A or B?

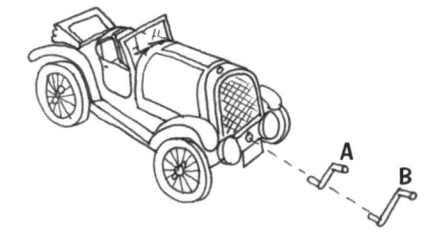

Q6 Below is a diagram of a crank and slider mechanism.
Copy and complete the diagram by adding the following labels:

 slider
 crank
 rotary motion
 connecting rod
 reciprocating motion

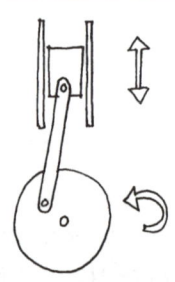

Section Four — Systems and Mechanisms

Levers and Links

Levers are used to help move or lift things. All simple levers have a load, a pivot and effort.

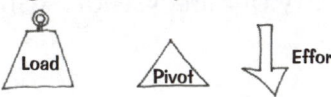

Q1 Sketch out a simple diagram to illustrate each of the following levers, and explain how they work by giving an example of each one.

   a) first class lever   b) second class lever   c) third class lever

Q2 Say what type of lever is used in each of the following examples.

   a) a wheelbarrow   d) a garden fork
   b) a fishing rod   e) opening a tin of paint with a screwdriver
   c) a crow bar

Q3 Which of the wheelbarrows below will be the easiest to lift, and why?

   a)   b)    c)

Q4 Say whether the following statements about double acting levers are true or false.

   a) A double acting lever, like a pair of scissors, is a second class lever.
   b) A double acting lever, like a pair of scissors, is a pair of first class levers.
   c) A double acting lever, like a pair of scissors, is a third class lever.

Q5 Copy and complete the sentences below using words from the box.

   a) A link is something that .... different parts of a .... together.
   b) A link can .... and change the ....
   c) A .... changes the direction of a force through 90°.
   d) .... use loads of levers all linked together.

   bell crank   connects
   transfer forces
   lazy tongs   mechanism
   direction of motion

So can I upgrade my wheelbarrow to a see-saw then?...

Remember all 3 classes of lever have a Load, a Pivot and an Effort. Then the difference between the three classes is just which one is in the middle. Use **PLE** — meaning a 1st class lever has the **P**ivot in the middle, a 2nd class has the **L**oad in the middle etc. Easy-peasy-lemon-squeezy.

Section Four — Systems and Mechanisms

Product Analysis

Q1 Give five reasons why designers carry out analysis of existing products.

Q2 Four important factors in product analysis are — function, form, ergonomics and environmental concerns. Write a short definition of each of these factors.

Q3 Aesthetics is the overall look of the product. List four features of a bookcase that might affect its aesthetic appeal.

Q4 Mind maps / spider diagrams / brainstorming are often used to carry out product analysis. Copy out the mind map nelow and write down eight other features you would look for in a camera.

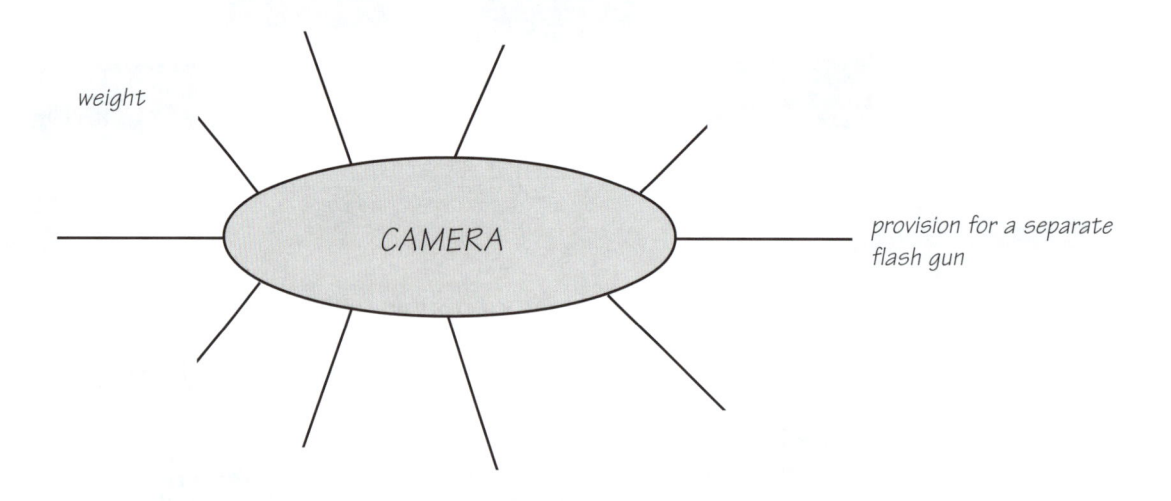

weight

CAMERA

provision for a separate flash gun

Q5 List four manufacturing processes you might find have been used in making a stapler.

Q6 Write a sentence to explain to someone what sub-assembly is. Give an example of sub-assembly you know about which would make it easier for someone else to understand the idea.

Eeeuuch — I just found a spider diagram in my bath...
Personally I don't think I'm a genius. Most people aren't. Which is why most designs are just rehashed versions of existing designs. Just like the charts are constantly plagued by remixes and dodgy cover versions... not that I'm suggesting Will and Gareth can't write songs of course, I'm sure they're just... um...

Quality Assurance and Control

Q1 Copy and complete the sentences below to show the difference between quality assurance and quality control.

  a) Quality assurance is about setting .... and then .... them.

  b) Quality control is how you .... to make sure you are .... those standards. Some suggested answers are given in the box below.

  Note — one word is used twice.

  | check | videos | set | missing | meeting | standards |

Q2 Say which of the following checks are essential elements of quality control and which aren't.

  a) The product meets its specification.
  b) Keeps the workforce fully occupied.
  c) The product will do the job it's meant for.
  d) The product meets all safety standards.
  e) Production lets advertising be worked out.
  f) The product meets all construction standards.
  g) The product ensures customer satisfaction.
  h) The product fits easily into its packaging.

Q3 Name the tool shown here and describe how it is used in quality control.

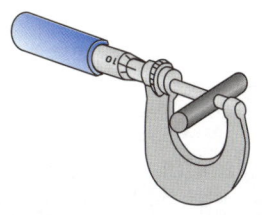

Q4 Sketch a 'go / not go' gauge (limit gauge) and give one advantage and one disadvantage it has over the tool in Q3, when checking components.

Q5 A shaft for a motor has to fit into an accurately bored hole of 20 mm diameter. Which of the below would be a suitable tolerance for the shaft?

  a) 20mm   + 0.05
            − 0.05

  b) 20mm   + 0.05
            − 0.00

  c) 20mm   + 0.00
            − 0.05

Q6 Say whether each of the following is an example of destructive testing or non-destructive testing.

  a) A company which makes light switches sets up a test rig to see how many times its switches can be operated before breaking.

  b) A company welding pipes to bring oil ashore from an oilrig sets up a system of checking the welds using x-rays.

Section Five — Market Influences

Social Responsibility

Q1 When designing products, manufacturers must be socially responsible. List four factors that a designer should take into consideration when designing a product in order to be socially responsible.

Q2 Copy and complete these sentences about social responsibility using words from the box.

a) A responsibly designed product should not harm the .... or the ....

b) For safety reasons, finishes used on products, such as varnish or ...., must not be ....

c) The manufacturing processes used must not produce toxic .... or .... waste.

d) Some .... or .... groups may be .... by the design and decoration of some products.

> toxic   harmful   cultural   environment
> religious   offended   user   emissions   paint

Q3 **Anthropometrics** is about the study and application of body size in product design. Name two different products where the use of anthropometrical data would be essential to the comfortable use of the product.

Q4 A badly-designed chair can cause health problems for someone who uses it every day. Give an example of one such possible health problem and suggest a modification to the chair's design which could help reduce the risk of this problem.

Q5 Name a material that is easy to recycle, so it can be re-used or made into another product.

Toxic emissions — my little brother knows all about them...
The problem is a lot of folks don't realise the value of recycling — after all, it doesn't improve the quality of products, and it's no cheaper for manufacturers. Plus it's a hassle separating your rubbish into glass, cans, paper, etc. But on the flipside, the whole planet's going down the pan if we don't. In a badly designed chair.

Section Five — Market Influences

Consumers

Q1 Consumers are essential to the manufacturing industry. Copy and complete the following sentences, using some of the words in the box.

Without .... there is no need for the ....

If no one buys the products, the .... will ....

| succeed | product | go bankrupt | customers | company | goats |

Q2 Say which of the following points are vital in promoting customer satisfaction.
   a) The product must be easy to use.
   b) The product must be fashionable.
   c) The product must be the cheapest on the market.
   d) The product advertising should be dynamic and colourful.
   e) The product should be good value for money.
   f) The product must be reliable and work well.

Q3 Copy and complete the following three key features of a system which would ensure customer satisfaction.
   a) Q...... Assurance
   b) Quality C ......
   c) Total Q...... M.........

Q4 There are several acts of Parliament to help ensure the safety and quality of products. Say which act promotes which aspect of product quality or safety.

   1) The Trades Description Act
   2) The Consumer Safety Act
   3) The Sale of Goods Act

   a) Ensures that products perform as they should and have a good life span.
   b) Ensures that any claim made by the manufacturer for its product is true.
   c) Legislates over fire regulations and specifications for clothes, toys, electrical equipment, etc.

Q5 What does it mean when a product is marked with the initials CE?

Q6 Name four agencies that consumers could go to in order to get help with dodgy goods.

Q7 Safety labels are often awarded to products that have met the relevant safety and design standards. Say what the following initials stand for.
   a) BSI
   b) BEAB

Section Five — Market Influences

The Environment

Q1 Copy and complete these sentences using words from the stupid looking box below.

    a) The 6,000,000,000,000 .... in the .... are using the Earth's .... at a frightening rate.

    b) We create too much .... and pollute water .... and the ....

              people   atmosphere   waste
              sources   resources   country
              water   world

Q2 Copy out the following list of resources, and for each one say whether it is "renewable" or "non-renewable". Also write "likely to run out" next to any that are predicted to become scarce, or to have run out, in your lifetime.

    a) natural gas   d) solar power   g) coal
    b) petroleum   e) timber (softwood)   h) paper
    c) wind power   f) metal ores   i) water

Q3 Draw the symbol which indicates a material can (and should) be recycled.

Q4 For each of the following, say whether they can or cannot be recycled.

    a) petroleum
    b) metal
    c) coal
    d) paper

Q5 How much of Britain's rubbish is recycled at present (to the nearest 10%)?

Q6 What percentage of waste should Britain aim to be recycling by the year 2016, according to European community guidelines?

Q7 A manufacturer is thinking of setting up a new factory. List three things he should consider doing to ensure his factory is environmentally friendly.

Section Five — Market Influences

Health and Safety

Q1   Say what safety gear should be worn or used when undertaking the following tasks.

   a)   handling thin metal

   b)   working with hot metal

   c)   sanding wood

   d)   hot metal casting

Q2   Working with machinery, whether fixed or portable, can be very dangerous. Copy and complete the sentences below using words in the box.

   a)   .... must be in place on lathes and drilling machines before starting the machine.

   b)   .... off and isolate a machine before carrying out any ....

   c)   .... the machine before walking away to do something else.

   d)   .... must be tied back when working to avoid entanglement.

   e)   Only .... on a machine, at a time, is a very good safety rule to follow.

   | stop | long hair | guards | adjustments | one person | switch |

Q3   Explain what a chuck key is, and what you must do with them before switching on machinery.

Q4   Name three ways of securing a piece of wood or metal while it is being worked on.

Q5   Describe the safety risks being demonstrated by the welder below and suggest suitable precautions he could take.

Safety first — a tip for life...
Most people don't like getting hurt. Think before you do something stupid and end up being responsible for someone else's injury and pain. Though at some point you'll probably have to dump someone and break their heart because you just don't fancy them anymore. My advice — eternal chastity and singleness.

Section Five — Market Influences

Health and Safety

Q1 Copy and complete the following sentences about safety considerations in product design. Use words from the predictable box below.

a) A coffee table must be .... enough to stand someone sitting on it without it ....

b) The .... of a pull-along toy must be securely fastened to the .... so that they cannot be pulled off and become a choking hazard.

c) A metal desk lamp must be electrically .... so that the user won't be ....

| electrocuted | collapsing | plastic wheels | strong | axles | earthed |

Q2 State three aspects of modern car design which help protect the driver from serious injury.

Q3 You have been asked to design a cuddly teddy bear for a young child. List three safety points you would need to consider.

Q4 List three safety features you would build into your designs for a set of stepladders.

Q5 Each of the bodies listed a) to e) is responsible for either: **approving product design, prosecuting suppliers of products which aren't safe**, or else they're **not directly responsible for product safety**. Copy out the list of bodies and say who does each of these things.

a) British Medical Council

b) Design Council

c) Trading Standards Offices

d) Department of Health and Social Security

e) British Electrotechnical Approvals Board

Section Five — Market Influences

Section Six — Industrial Awareness

Scale of Production

Q1 'Scale of production' is all about the quantity of products that you are going to manufacture. Copy and complete the summary table using the sentences below.

Non-stop production 24hrs / day.

Down time is unproductive and needs to be kept to a minimum.

You need a large, unskilled workforce.

Examples include oil and chemical manufacture.

Batches can be repeated as many times as required.

Making a single, one-off product.

Made to meet the customer's individual and specific requirements.

Making products on a really large scale.

The machinery and labour used need to be flexible.

Labour intensive, and requires a highly skilled workforce.

The specialised equipment required is very expensive.

The specialised equipment required is very expensive.

Making a specific quantity of a product.

Examples include one-off buildings, e.g. The Millennium Dome.

Different stages are broken down into simple repetitive tasks.

Type of Production	List of Key Facts
Jobbing Production	
Batch production	
Mass Production	
Continuous Production	

Q2 During your GCSE project you will make a single product. Write down what category of production this comes under and explain your answer.

Q3 How does the scale of production affect the cost of the end product? Write a short paragraph to explain your answer, using a car as an example.

Mass production — 20 000 Hail Marys every day...

In an exam they'll either ask you for examples of the different types of production, or to identify which type applies to a given situation. The only way to be sure of sailing through is to learn the key points for each type <u>as well as a few example situations</u> for each one.

Manufacturing Systems

Q1 Copy and complete the following sentences about cell production. Use the words from the box below to fill in the gaps.

    a) Cell production is where the manufacture of a product is .... in to individual components, each made by a different .... of people, called a ....

    b) Within each cell the team is .... for all aspects of the production of their ...., including .... control and .... of the machines.

    c) The main .... of this method include..............., good .... and high quality of the finished product.

| team | quality | communication | responsible | advantages |
| teamwork | maintenance | component | cell | split |

Q2 In-line assembly is used in the mass production of cars. Explain why mainly unskilled labour is used.

Q3 What does F.M.S. stand for in manufacturing? Explain how it works.

Q5 What does J.I.T. stand for? Explain what this system involves and what main advantages it has.

A manufacturing system — what, like the UK pop music industry...

When you're learning about these different manufacturing systems, try to learn a specific example for each one which you could use in an exam question. Maybe you could learn examples sung to a tune — "It's murder on the factory floor, so you'd better not kill the FMS approach to batch production, DJ..."

Section Six — Industrial Awareness

CAD/CAM and CIM in Industry

Q1 What does CAD stand for, and what does it refer to?

Q2 What does CAM stand for, and what does it refer to?

Q3 CAD/CAM is the process of joining CAD and CAM systems together. Explain how this is done.

Q4 Copy and complete the following sentences. Use words on the screen on the right to fill in the blanks.

a) CIM is the system by which different .... of the .... are .... together by a central ....

b) CIM helps to .... different stages in the design process, and the central computer system makes .... easy.

c) The really clever bit is the ...., that will automatically .... any changes made and will alert all related stages. This can save a lot of .... and eliminate costly ....

Words on screen: process, linked, mistakes, stages, update, software, coordinate, communication, computer system, time

Q5 It's easy to get confused with all these different abbreviations. Copy out and complete these headings. After you've done that, say which numbered point below matches each of parts a) to e). I've done the first one for you.

a) CAD — Computer-A*ided* D*esign* = *point 3*

b) CAM — Computer-A............. M.............

c) CAD/CAM — Computer-A............. D............. A............. M.............

d) CIM — Computer I............. M.............

e) CNC — Computer N............. C.............

1) process of joining CAD and CAM systems together
2) computer software which controls manufacturing machines
3) designing using computers
4) central computer system linking different stages of the design process
5) manufacturing using computer controlled machines

Section Six — Industrial Awareness

Advertising and Marketing

Q1 Say which of these descriptions goes with which appropriate person within the design process.

a) Identifies a need, gives the designer a clear brief, carries out market research and raises money for the project.
b) Develops the client's ideas, sets out a specification and produces detailed working drawings of the final design.
c) Plans and carries out manufacturing, safely and efficiently, to produce consistent results and make a profit.
d) Gives the customer what they want, at an affordable price.
e) Gets a high quality product that works, fulfils a need and is good value for money.

1) designer
2) retailer
3) client
4) user
5) manufacturer

Q2 Write a sentence to explain what the initials "BSI" stands for, and what BSI does.

Q3 Sketch out the BSI Kitemark, and explain what it represents.

Q4 What is ISO 9000?

Q5 All adverts have the main aim of influencing people, trying to convince them to buy a particular product. Write out a list of five different forms of advertising media.

Q6 Market research is often carried out in the form of a questionnaire or survey. What is the point of doing market research?

Q7 What makes a good questionnaire? Copy the table below and put the following points into the correct columns.

brief questions
inoffensive questions
long questions
too many questions
multiple choice questions
relevant and clear questions
irrelevant information
open ended questions
questions where the answers are easy to use and analyse
tick boxes

Things to Include	Things to Avoid

Section Six — Industrial Awareness

Good Working Practice

Q1   Describe briefly what a flow chart is.

Q2   All flow charts are made up from a series of standard symbols.
     Copy and complete these sentences with words in the box.

   a)   .... is used for the start and finish of a flow chart.
   b)   .... is used to show a process or action.
   c)   .... is used for decisions or questions.
   d)   .... is used to link any of the stages together.

> a rectangle
> an arrow
> a diamond
> a sausage shape

Q3   Draw a flow chart of the following stages of making a cup of coffee.
     Use the correct symbols and link up all stages with arrows. Your chart
     must include the actions and decisions listed below.

   Actions: Fill kettle with water and turn on.
              Put instant coffee into mug.
              Add boiling water.
              Add milk.
              Add sugar, stir and taste.

   Decisions: Does it taste sweet enough?

Q4   Quality control can be easily built in to a flow chart. The example below
     shows a section of a flow chart for making a child's toy. It is essential that
     the shapes are made to fit snugly into the holes in the box. Copy and
     complete the chart below, filling in missing sections and arrows.

   Missing Text From Flowchart:

   Discard shape and start again.

   Sand down shape to correct size.

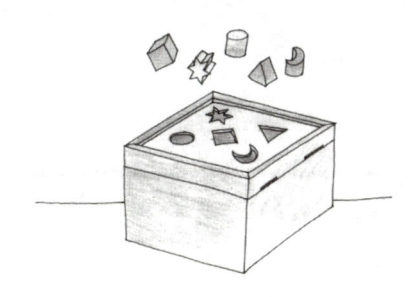

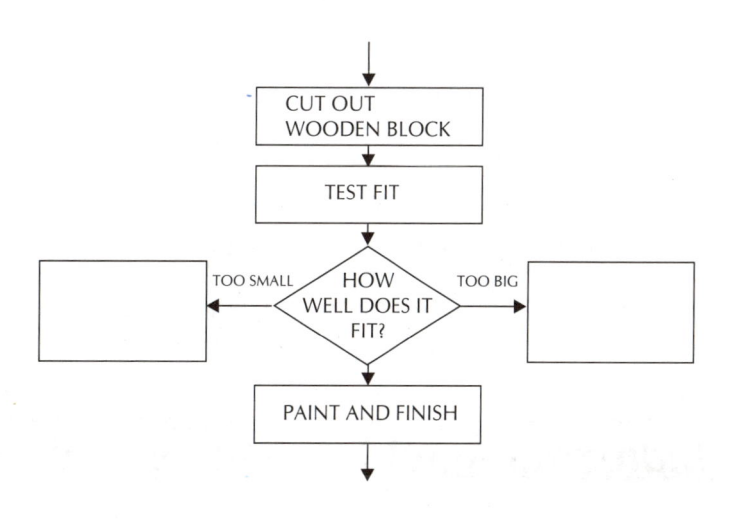

Flowchart:
CUT OUT WOODEN BLOCK → TEST FIT → HOW WELL DOES IT FIT? (TOO SMALL / TOO BIG) → PAINT AND FINISH

Section Six — Industrial Awareness

Jigs, Moulds and Templates

Q1 Describe what a template is, and explain why it is important that it is strong and hardwearing.

Q2 a) Describe and sketch how a drilling jig could help drill a series of holes along a piece of wood.

   b) List two advantages of using a jig, instead of marking out the holes and drilling them by hand?

Q3 Copy and complete these sentences about moulds, using words in the box.

   a) .... are commonly used in ....manufacturing, in processes like ....

   b) Once an ....mould has been made, detailed plastics shapes can be formed with it ....again.

   c) Industrial moulds are .... to produce, so a manufacturer needs to be .... of their design, and needs to be able to make .... numbers of their product to make it cost-effective.

   | plastics | large | vacuum forming | over and over |
   | moulds | certain | accurate | expensive |

Q4 Write down which of the following statements are true and which are false.

   a) A jig is a kind of clamp.

   b) A template needs to be strong and hardwearing so it can be used repetitively.

   c) Moulds help in the production of 3-D plastic shapes.

   d) Jigs come in different shapes and sizes and are usually made specifically for a particular job.

   e) Templates are commonly used in plastics manufacturing, in processes such as vacuum forming.

Industrial mould — like normal mould only more shiny...

Try not to get confused between jigs and templates. A template is normally a simple shape that you draw round to reproduce identical shapes. Jigs are often more complicated and help to simplify a particular part of the production process.

Section Six — Industrial Awareness

GCSE Design & Technology

Resistant Materials

CGP   Answers

Contents

Section One — The Design Process 3

Section Two — Tools and Processes 5

Section Three — Materials and Components 7

Section Four — Systems and Mechanisms 10

Section Five — Market Influences 11

Section Six — Industrial Awareness 13

Answers: P.1 — P.4

Section 1 — The Design Process

Page 1 — Design Brief

Q1 Any reasonable answers, e.g. companies carry out customer research to ensure people will need their products and want to buy them.

Q2 Any reasonable answers, e.g. a design brief is a description of why a product is needed and the problem it will solve. It should include a description of how this product will meet the need, how it will be used and the environment that it will be used in.

Q3 Any sensible answers, e.g.
   a) A CD storage unit.
   b) A storage system that holds a collection of makeup in order.
   c) A key fob that makes a noise when they talk or whistle to make the keys easy to find.

Q4 Any reasonable answers, e.g.
   a) There are problems with an existing design.
   b) The performance of an existing design could be improved.
   c) There is a gap in the market that needs to be filled.

Q5 Any reasonable answers, e.g.
   a) identifying a need — finding a problem that can be solved by designing an object.
   b) gap in the market — when there is a demand for a product that is not available.
   c) consumer research — finding out people's likes and dislikes.
   d) user group — target market. The people you want to buy and use your product.
   e) environment — where the object will be used.

Page 2 — Research

Q1 Any reasonable answers, e.g. whether people will want your product; what makes an existing product good or bad; what materials, pre-manufactured components, techniques and processes you want to use; how much your product should cost; ideas and starting points for your designs.

Q2 a) Internet — secondary
   b) questionnaires — primary
   c) letters — primary
   d) interviews — primary
   e) books — secondary
   f) magazines — secondary
   g) newspapers — secondary

Q3

Method of Research	Use
Questionnaires	Tells you about people's likes and dislikes. This will help you to identify market trends and your target group.
Disassembling an existing product	Tells you how a current product is made and how it works. It will help you decide which materials and processes you need to use and how your product will meet consumers' needs.
Measuring existing products	Gives you an idea of the weight, size and shape of your product, and its sensory features.

Q4 research analysis

Page 3 — Design Specification

Q1 Any reasonable answer, e.g. A design specification is a list of requirements that the final product must meet.

Q2 e.g.

(spider diagram with "design specification" at centre linked to: cost, material, size, shape, function, ergonomics, anthropometrics (body measurement data), durability, maintenance, finish, manufacturing processes)

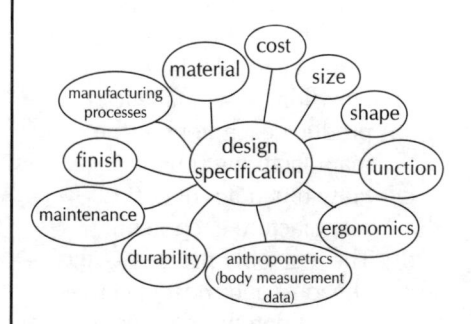

Q3

Term	Meaning
durability	how long the product will last
maintenance	concerns repair when product fails
dimensions	the measurements
function	the product's job
appearance	what shape, colour, texture etc. will be most suitable

Q4 a) office lamp — to be designed so that it is free standing and suitable for a professional environment
   b) cosmetic mirror — designed to be transportable, to fit in a pocket or bag
   c) disposable lady shaver — designed for a female, must be replaced after use
   d) computer mouse — must be ergonomically designed so that it is comfortable to hold and use

Q5 Any reasonable answer, e.g.
- must hold a certain number of cds
- free standing or wall mounted or both
- designed so that cd labels are clearly visible
- designed to attract a large market
- strong and durable
- aesthetically pleasing
- maintenance free

Page 4 — Generating Proposals

Q1 Any reasonable answers, e.g.
   a) mood board — a collection of images, mounted on a board, that are linked to the intended product or user of the product. It is used to help to trigger ideas in designing.
   b) brainstorming — when a designer or group of people pool key words, questions and initial thoughts relating to the product they're designing. Brainstorming allows you write down lots of possible ideas and think about all your options.
   c) an existing product — a product that is already on the market. Changing features of an existing product, or the production methods used to make an existing product, can help to spur your own ideas.

GCSE Resistant Materials Workbook — The Answers

Answers: P.5 — P.8

Q2 annotation.

Q3 Any five of the following: materials, appearance, the intended user, joining techniques, functions, advantages and disadvantages of it's features, production method, cost.

Q4 Any reasonable answer, e.g.

Presentation Technique	Description
orthograhic projection	diagrams showing the 2D views of a 3D product
digital camera photos	obvious really...
cross-sections	diagrams showing the product as it would look if it was sliced down the middle
freehand sketching	sketches done without the aid of designing materials — they give an impression of the features of the product
perspective drawing	drawings that show objects head on, or from an angle, to give a realistic picture of what the object will look like — grid paper is used to make the object look like it is getting smaller in the distance

Page 5 — Development

Q1 Any of the following: colour, joints, size, ergonomics, anthropometrics, function, additional features, etc.

Q2 A prototype. It allows you to try out different aspects of your design, break your design down into smaller, more manageable parts, and identify problems in your design before you've spent too much time or money on it. Prototypes are also useful for testing reactions to your design.

Q3 Any three of the following: photos, working drawings, sketches, graphs, tables, charts

Q4 Once you have developed your designs using sketches, models or tests, you need to analyse the results. This will allow you make modifications to your design and improve the product, or make it ready for mass production. It is also important that the design is checked to ensure that it meets the design specification.

Page 6 — Evaluation

Q1 Any three of the following: material testing, questionnaires, interviews, giving trial products to a group of intended users, comparing and contrasting existing products

Q2 Any reasonable answer, e.g. five of the following:
1. Does the product work well?
2. Does the product look good?
3. Are you unsure about any of the features?
4. Would you buy this product if it were on the market?
5. How much are you prepared to pay?
6. Do you prefer another similar product to this one?

Q3 Product 1 (mechanical whisk):
function — to mix ingredients together
ergonomics — plastic handles for comfort, lightweight so easy to carry, horizontal handle (at top) could make it difficult to hold still while whisking
appearance — grey, metallic, basic shape
Product 2 (electric whisk):
function — to mix ingredients together
ergonomics — electric so minimum effort, large handle for comfort, button on top for ease of operation
appearance — white to blend in with most kitchen environments, plastic casing to protect electrical circuits

Q4 a) The materials, tools and equipment that they will need, and their availability.
b) How long it will take to produce each item — the manufacturing time.
c) How much it will cost to manufacture each item.
d) The assembly process — the cheapest and most effective way of putting the product together. This will be important when planning for production.

Page 7 — Manufacturer's Specification

Q1 A manufacturer's specification is a list of specific points that tell the manuafcturer exactly how the product will be made.

Q2 Working drawings are detailed drawn plans of the product being made. They show precise dimension and tolerances etc.

Q3 using a spreadsheet

Q4 a) Clear construction details — explaining exactly how each piece is going to be made.
b) Sizes — precise measurements of each part.
c) Tolerances — the maximum and minimum sizes of each part.
d) Finishing details — any special sequencing for finishing.
e) Quality control instructions — where and how the manufacturing process should be checked.
f) Costings — how much each part costs, and details of other costs involved.

Page 8 — Planning Production

Q1 Charts will help you to plan how long each stage of the production process will take and how each stage will fit into the total time. Charts help you to make your product as quickly and efficiently as possible.

Q2 Any reasonable answer, e.g.
A Gantt chart is a time plan that helps you to organise your tasks. The tasks are written down one side of the table and time along the top. The table is filled with coloured squares, which show how long each task takes and the order they're done in.

GCSE Resistant Materials Workbook — The Answers

Answers: P.9 — P.12

Q3 [Flow chart symbols: Start/End (oval), Decision (diamond), Process (rectangle)]

Q4 Any reasonable answer, e.g.
A summative evaluation is a final report on the product being designed. It is a summary of the product and what you've learnt. A summative evaluation involves: Examining how well the product works and how well it meets the design specification. It could include tests, questionnaires or surveys and a description of what you would do differently if you were to make the product again.

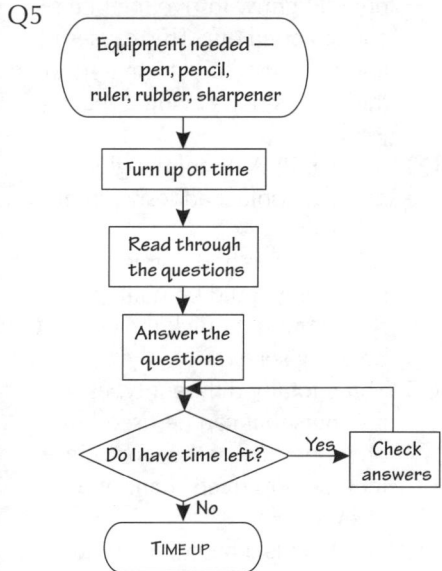

Q5 [Flow chart:
Equipment needed — pen, pencil, ruler, rubber, sharpener →
Turn up on time →
Read through the questions →
Answer the questions →
Do I have time left? — Yes → Check answers; No → TIME UP]

Section 2 — Tools and Processes

Page 9 — Hand Tools

Q1 coping saw
Q2 a fine-cut flat file
Q3 Before <u>removing material</u> always <u>mark out</u> carefully and then double <u>check</u> your accuracy. Use suitable tools like bench <u>planes</u>, files, wood <u>chisels</u>, drill bits, <u>gougers</u> and saws.

Q4 a) False
b) True
c) True
d) False
e) True

Q5 a) Wood or Plastic
b) Wood
c) Wood
d) Metal or Plastic
e) Wood

Q6 a cold chisel.

Page 10 — Machine and Power Tools

Q1 a) False
b) True
c) False
d) True
e) False

Q2 Lathes are often used for turning and cutting materials to make them round in cross section or cylindrical.

Q3 A sanding disc is used to accurately shape woods, metals and plastics, especially for trimming to a line.

Q4 A (bench) grinder

Q5 A milling machine (or other sensible answer)

Q6 Any sensible answer, e.g. it has interchangeable blades, it has variable speeds, it has thin blades which can easily move round curves.

Q7 A <u>power planer</u> is used to remove <u>shavings of wood</u>. It can be used for a smooth finish or for <u>rough shaping</u>. It has the advantage that it is <u>faster</u> than a bench plane and needs <u>less effort</u>.

Page 11 — Deforming

Q1 Deforming woods and metals means changing the shape of the materials.

Q2 b) laminating

Q3 Any sensible answer e.g. by folding sheet metal.

Q4 A door knocker could be forged by heating the iron red hot, then hammering into shape on an anvil.

Q5 The acrylic could be placed over a strip heater until softened along the line, along which the acrylic can then be bent.

Q6 press moulding

Q7 Any reasonable answers e.g.
The plastic takes the shape of the inside of the mould which is then opened to remove the product, as below:

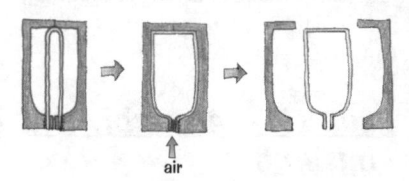

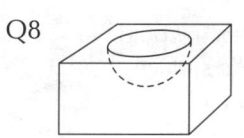

[Diagram showing blow moulding process with air injection]

Q8 [Diagram of block with bowl-shaped mould]

Q9 former, mould, plastic powder, high temperature, pressure

Page 12 — Reforming

Q1 Any sensible answer e.g.
die casting is a process used to mould metals and thermoplastics. The material is melted and poured into the mould which is in the shape of the product.

Q2 An example of a simple flow chart is shown below.

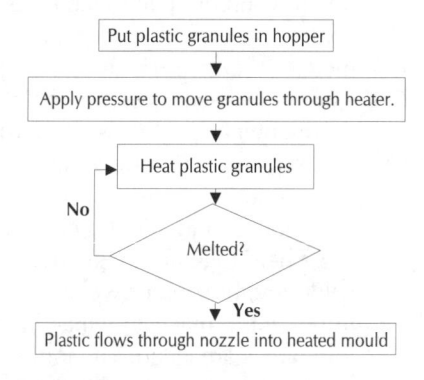

[Flow chart:
Put plastic granules in hopper →
Apply pressure to move granules through heater →
Heat plastic granules →
Melted? — No (loop back); Yes →
Plastic flows through nozzle into heated mould]

Q3 Injection moulding and extrusion are both automatic and continuous.

Answers: P.13 — P.15

Q4

plastic granules are fed by a screw into the heater then forced out of the nozzle

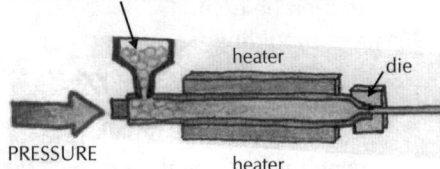

Q5 any sensible answer, e.g. resin casting
Q6 extrusion

Page 13 — Assembly and Finishing

Q1 A good sequence would be:
   b) sand inside surface
   a) put glue in joints
   e) clamp box together
   g) fit top and bottom
   i) sand outside surfaces
   d) cut box into two parts
   c) fit hinges
   f) varnish outside surfaces
   h) line inside with fabric
   NB alternatively the hinges could be fitted after varnishing, to avoid getting varnish on them.
Q2 A good sequence could be:
   clean up with glass paper
   paint with primer and rub down when dry
   paint with undercoat and rub down when dry paint with gloss coat
Q3 metals
Q4 'A dry run' means assembling a product without glue as a trial run.
Q5 Any sensible answer e.g. sash cramps and G-cramps.
Q6 If the joints of the final product are to be held together by gluing, soldering, brazing or welding, it is important to make sure that all the joint areas are clean. The joints must not be touched after they have been cleaned because greasy fingerprints can stop the joint from working.

Page 14 — Fabricating — Screws and Bolts

Q1 Fabricating means the joining of pieces using the most appropriate method.
Q2 A machine screw is threaded along all of its length while a bolt is threaded along only a part of the length. Also, bolts have different shaped heads from machine screws (square or hexagonal), and are tightened with spanners instead of screwdrivers.
Q3

Fastener	Fact
self-tapping screws	have hardened threads
screws and bolts	are plated with zinc, brass or chrome
woodscrews	require pilot and clearance holes

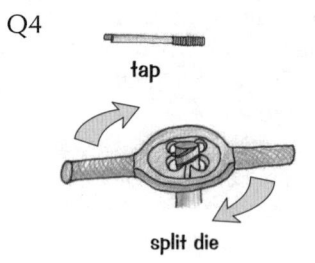

Q4

Q5 A female thread is found around the inside of a hole while a male thread is made around the outside of a round bar or rod.
Q6 a) A round rod can be made to fit a threaded hole by cutting a male thread onto the rod.
   b) Bolts are tightened with spanners.
   c) A tap is used to cut a female thread.
   d) Bolts and machine screws are used with washers and nuts.
   e) Self-tapping screws are designed to cut their own threaded holes.
   f) A split die is used to cut a male thread.
Q7

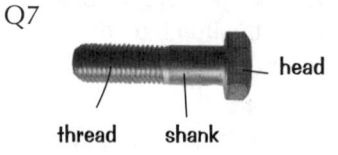

Page 15 — Fabricating — Nails, Rivets and Adhesives

Q1 a) The top and bottom could be fixed on using glue and panel pins. The pins would be punched below the surface of the wood using a nail punch.
   b) The small indents would be filled with wood filler and then sanded smooth before painting.
Q2 A hole is drilled in the metal pieces being joined. The metal pin is inserted through a hole in the centre of the pop rivet. Both rivet and pin are placed in the hole in the material. The pin is pulled tight with riveting pliers and snapped off. This causes the end to expand and form a head on the other side, leaving a secure joint.
Q3 a) e.g. PVA or animal glue
   b) e.g. contact adhesive or epoxy resin
Q4 A joining method that is quick but not strong could be nailing. A strong but not quick method could be using screws.
Q5 Three totally different types of fasteners that can be used from only one side of the work piece include pop rivets, nails and screws.
Q6 a) A set is a hammer-like tool used for riveting.
   b) Epoxy resin is a type of adhesive.
   c) Nails are only used in wood.
   d) The head of a nail can be hidden below the surface using a nail punch.
   e) Adhesives are often used to reinforce other methods of fabrication.
   f) Pop rivets are a quick and easy method of joining sheet metal.

GCSE Resistant Materials Workbook — The Answers

Answers: P.16 — P.20

Page 16 — Joints

Q1 a) mitred joint
    b) mortise and tenon joint
    c) dovetail joint
    d) butt joint
    e) dowel joint
    f) housing joint
    g) halving joint
    h) lap joint
Q2 The act of cutting joints increases the gluing surface area and make the joining stronger.
Q3 knock-down fittings.
Q4 c) knock-down joint
    b) glued butt joint
    a) glued dovetail joint
Q5 Any reasonable answers, e.g.

Joint	Use
dovetail	drawer construction
mitred	picture frames
mortise and tenon	tables and chairs
butt	cheap shelving
knock-down	flat-pack furniture
housing	shelving

Page 17 — Joining Metals

Q1 soft soldering, hard soldering, welding, silver soldering or brazing
Q2 1. Thoroughly clean the metal.
    2. Ensure the joint is well fitting with minimal gaps.
    3. Apply flux to the joint area.
    4. When the metal is hot enough, apply the spelter and allow to melt into the joint.
Q3 soldering
Q4 Flux helps to stop the air oxidising the surface of the metal.
Q5 a) True
    b) False
    c) True
    d) False
    e) False
    f) True
    g) True
    h) False

Page 18 — Computerised Production

Q1 Any sensible answers e.g. CAD allows designers to draw, make changes and compare designs quickly and cheaply.
Q2 The advantages include being able to view the object from many angles, change the scale of the components, quickly change dimensions and view the object in different colour schemes.
Q3 Computer numerically controlled means that the program works out the necessary movements of the machine. It then sends data to the machine in the form of numbers for the microprocessor to interpret and act upon.
Q4 Any sensible answers, e.g.

Advantages	Disadvantages
less cost due to less need for specialised machines	special purpose machines are cheaper for large scale production
less chance of human error	high initial cost
easy, quick and cheap to change machine	high cost of training

Q5 CAD enables the drawing to be converted into digital data to be distributed electronically to other teams of people working on the project.
Q6 CAD can be used to send information to machines on a production line. This is called <u>Computer-Aided Manufacture</u>. CAM machines are <u>Computer Numerically Controlled</u> and have onboard <u>computer</u> processors that interpret the CAD <u>data</u> and control the movement of the <u>tool head</u>.

Section 3 — Materials and Components

Page 19 — Properties of Materials

Q1 1) <u>Tensile</u>
    2) <u>Compressive</u>
    3) <u>Bending</u>
    4) <u>Shear</u>
    5) <u>Torsional</u>
Q2 Any reasonable answer, e.g. Hardness is the ability to withstand abrasive wear and tear, denting and bending.
Q3 It is said to have good plastic qualities.
Q4 It will crack or break easily.
Q5 Tough
Q6 Durable
Q7 Any reasonable answers, e.g.

Property:	Example Product:
hardness	drills and files
plasticity	a flexible plastic ruler
brittleness	glass and acrylic
toughness	bulletproof vests
durability	concrete

Page 20 — Metals

Q1 a) ferrous
    b) non-ferrous
    c) ferrous
    d) non-ferrous
Q2 Any reasonable answer, e.g.

Ferrous Metal:	Properties:	Example Uses:
Mild Steel	quite strong and cheap, but rusts easily	nuts and bolts
High-Carbon Steel	harder than mild steel, and can be hardened	drills and files
Stainless Steel	hard and will not rust, but can be expensive	sinks and cutlery

GCSE Resistant Materials Workbook — The Answers

Answers: P.21 — P.23

Q3 Any reasonable answers, e.g.

Non-Ferrous Metal:	Properties:	Example uses:
Aluminium	lightweight and corrosion resistant	drinks cans
Brass	malleable, ductile and attractive	door handles
Copper	soft and malleable, and conducts electricity	pipes

Q4 Any reasonable answer, e.g. An alloy is a mixture of two or more metals, or a metal mixed together with another element. They are made in order to produce metals with different properties or characteristics. Alloys may be (for example) stronger or more resistant to corrosion than a pure metal.

Q5 a) False
b) False
c) True
d) False
e) True

Page 21 — Metals

Q1 Any reasonable answer, e.g.
1) <u>Annealing</u> is when a metal is softened by heating and then left to cool.
2) <u>Hardening</u> is the process of heating a metal and then rapidly cooling it.
3) <u>Tempering</u> is when a metal is heated in order to make it tougher.

Q2

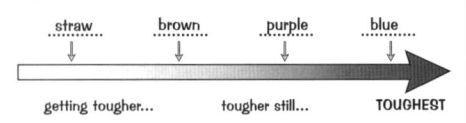

straw → brown → purple → blue
getting tougher... tougher still... TOUGHEST

Q3 Any reasonable answer, e.g.
1) <u>Cleaning</u> — any metal you're painting must be thoroughly cleaned beforehand. This can be done with paraffin or white spirit. If a lot of dirt or rust needs to be cleaned off you may need to use a wire brush, or emery cloth.
2) <u>Primer</u> — when painting steel, you need to use a primer such as red oxide or zinc chromate, so that the layers of paint aren't absorbed by the metal.
3) <u>Top Coat</u> — to give high protection and a good quality of finish, you need to put on a durable top coat such as hammerite.

Q4 Any reasonable answer, e.g. Plastic coating is a thin layer of plastic which covers the metal. To apply it you need to heat up the metal evenly (in an oven) and then plunge it into fluidised powder. You then return the metal to the oven in order to fuse the plastic to the surface.

Q5 Polishing can be carried out by <u>hand</u> or by using a <u>buffing wheel</u>, which is coated with an abrasive <u>polish</u>. The metal is then polished until the required <u>surface</u> finish is achieved.

Q6 Lacquering provides a barrier against tarnishing and oxidising. It is often used on decorative items such as jewellery (or any other reasonable example).

Page 22 — Plastics

Q1 Any three of the following:
a) Thermoplastics are recyclable, thermosetting plastics are not.
b) Thermosetting plastics resist heat, thermoplastics don't.
c) Thermoplastics can be easily formed in to shapes and they have plastic memory.
d) Thermosetting plastics undergo a chemical change when heated so that they become hard and rigid.

Q2

Thermoplastics	Thermosetting Plastics
acrylic ABS polystyrene polythene	melemine-formaldehyde polyester resin epoxy resin ureaformaldehyde

Q3 Any three of each of the following two lists:
plastics before processing — powders, granules, pellets, liquids
processed plastics — films, sheets, rods, tubes and extruded mouldings

Q4 Plastics don't need a protective surface finish because they already have a high resistance to corrosion and decay.

Q5 e.g. using wet and dry paper, abrasive polish, antistatic cream, a buffing machine, etc.

Q6 Plastizote is a closed cell polythene foam. It's great because it has eliminated the need for toxic chemicals which are currently used within the foam industry.

Page 23 — Wood

Q1 Any reasonable answer, e.g.

Discription of Category	Softwoods come from coniferous (cone bearing) trees. They typically have thin, needle-like leaves and are evergreen.
Rate of Growth	fast growing, reaching maturity within 30 years
Cost (in relation to Hardwoods)	cheaper than hardwoods
Three Examples	pine, cedar, yew, etc.

Q2 Any reasonable answer, e.g.

Description of Category	Hardwoods are mostly broadleaved trees which shed their leaves annually (deciduous).
Rate of Growth	slow growing, reaching maturity in about 100 years
Cost (in relation to Softwoods)	generally more expensive than softwoods
Three Examples	mahogany, beech, oak, elm, etc

Q3 1. b)
2. c)
3. e)
4. a)
5. d)

GCSE Resistant Materials Workbook — The Answers

Answers: P.24 — P.27

Page 24 — Manufactured Boards

Q1 a) plywood
    b) blockboard
    c) laminboard
    d) MDF
    e) chipboard

Q2 Any reasonable answer, e.g.
    1) They are very strong (especially plywood).
    2) They're a lot cheaper than solid wood.
    3) They are available in large sizes, because you're not restricted by the size of the tree.

Q3 Having the grain direction alternating on each layer increases the strength of the material.

Q4 You couldn't buy the board in picture c. It contains 6 layers. Normally you can only buy plywood with an odd number of layers.

Q5 In both of these examples, strips of softwood are glued together, side by side, and then sandwiched between two veneers on each side. The difference between the two is that laminboard contains softwood strips that are between 5 and 7mm wide, where as blockboard contains softwood strips that are between 7 and 25mm wide.

Q6 Medium Density Fibreboard.

Q7 Chipboard is produced by compressing wood particles together with glue. It can be made stronger by adding hardwood or plastic veneered surfaces.

Page 25 — Composites and Smart Materials

Q1 A material that is formed from two or more materials bonded together.

Q2 Mechanical and other properties are improved in composite materials, resulting in improved strength to weight ratios.

Q3 Any reasonable answers, e.g.
    a) Tufnol is made from woven linen impregnated with phenolic resin. It can be used in gears and bearings.
    b) Glass Reinforced Plastic (GRP) is a plastic material with glass fibre strands that give it greater strength. It is often used to make boats and car bodies.
    c) Carbon Fibre is a plastic material with carbon fibres bonded in to it. It's a very strong and lightweight material, often used in racing cars and protective helmets.

Q4 Any reasonable answer, e.g. Nitinol is a shape memory alloy. It can be easily shaped when cool, but returns to a remembered shape when heated above a certain temperature.

Q5 e.g. chips in computers

Q6 Silicon is a semiconductor. This means that its resistance decreases as its temperature increases. Single crystals of silicon are cut into thin wafers and have transistors etched onto the surface. A large chip of 20 cm diameter can contain up to one thousand million circuit elements.

Page 26 — Fittings and Fixtures

Q1 a) Butt Hinge — common hinge used on doors, set into the frame and door.
    b) Flush Hinge — screwed directly onto the surface of the wood. Easy to fit and used on lightweight jobs.
    c) Tee Hinges — long strap allows the hinge to support greater weight. Often used outside on things like garden sheds and gates.
    d) Pivot Hinges — the hinge is made from two separate parts which come apart so that you can, for example, easily lift a door off its frame.

Q2 a) True
    b) False
    c) True
    d) False

Q3 1) Cupboard locks — these would enable the door to be locked shut.
    2) Catches — a catch simply holds a door closed without locking it. They are available in different types including magnetic and spring and ball catches.

Q4 They are suitable because they are all strong and hardwearing. Plated steel and brass can have highly decorative finishes.

Q5 Shelving fitments allow a shelf to be simply placed into position. No cutting is required and the shelves can be easily repositioned at any time.

Q6 The mortise and tenon joint is very strong, but takes time and skill to cut out and fit correctly.
    Leg fastenings are a lot quicker, offer extra reinforcement, and can be easily taken apart and put back together.

Page 27 — Adhesives

Q1 Polyvinyl Acetate

Q2 Any reasonable answer, e.g. Interior PVA will join wood as long as it doesn't get wet. Exterior PVA is more expensive and is able to join wood in wet conditions.

Q3 The right way to apply it is to...
    b) ...apply glue to both surfaces and wait about 10 minutes until the surfaces are tacky. Then bring the surfaces together and they will be stuck instantly.

Q4 Epoxy resin

Q5 It will stick together almost anything. The disadvantages are the cost and the mess you have to make in mixing it together.

Q6 It will easily stick to your skin so you need to avoid getting it on your fingers.

Q7 Acrylic cement (Tensol)

Answers: P.28 — P.32

Section 4 — Systems and Mechanisms

Page 28 — Systems

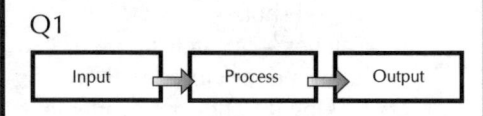

Q1 Input → Process → Output

Q2 The input is the movement of their legs. The process involved is the turning of the pedals, which in turn moves the chain, sprockets and wheels. Finally, the output is simply the forward motion of the bike.

Q3 The wheels and frame form a structural subsystem.
The pedals and gears form a mechanical subsystem.
The breaks form a mechanical or pneumatic subsystem.

Q4 mechanical advantage
Any reasonable example accepted — e.g. car jack, crow bar

Q5 a) linear motion
b) rotary motion
c) oscillating motion
d) reciprocating motion

Page 29 — Gear Mechanisms

Q1 Driver gear and driven gear. The driver gear is turned by hand or a motor (the input). This turns the driven gear (the output). They will turn in opposite directions.

Q2 a) anticlockwise
b) clockwise
c) clockwise
d) anticlockwise

Q3 the gear ratio

Q4 a) rack and pinion gears
b) bevel gears
c) compound gears
d) worm gears

Q5 Any reasonable diagrams, e.g.
a)
b)
c)
d)

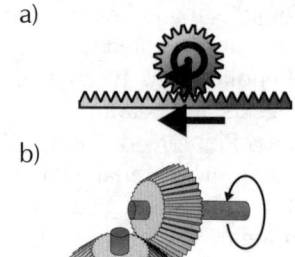

Page 30 — Belt Drives, Chains and Pulleys

Q1 A — motor shaft
B — drill shaft
C — flexible belt drive

Q2 Any reasonable answer, e.g. An example of a chain and sprocket mechanism is on a bike. It consists of two sprockets (toothed wheels) linked with a chain, which is made up from loads of links.

Q3 A chain and sprocket mechanism will not slip, whereas a belt drive can.

Q4
RPM of the driven pulley = (RPM of the driver pulley × diameter of the driver pulley) / diameter of the driven pulley

Q5 a) fastest position = A
b) slowest position = D

Q6 a) True
b) False
c) True
d) True

Page 31 — Gears and Belt Drives — Calculations

Q1 a) Driven gear will do 1/2 a turn.
b) Driven gear will do 2 turns.
c) Driven gear will do 1/3 a turn.
d) Driven gear will do 1 turn.
e) Driven gear will do 4 turns.

Q2 a) Driven RPM = 250
b) Driven RPM = 75
c) Driven RPM = 100
d) Driven RPM = 175
e) Driven RPM = 40

Page 32 — Cams and Cranks

Q1 A cam and <u>follower</u> convert <u>rotary</u> motion into <u>reciprocating</u> motion.

Q2 a) True
b) False
c) False
d) False

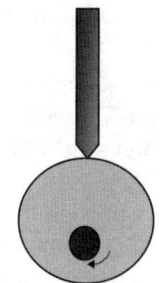

Q3 a) Motion: up and down in a uniform reciprocating motion

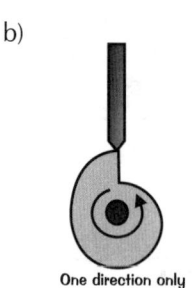

b) One direction only
Motion: gently rises and then suddenly drops

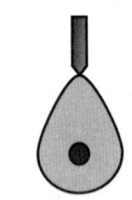

c) Motion: gently rises and falls

Answers: P.33 — P.34

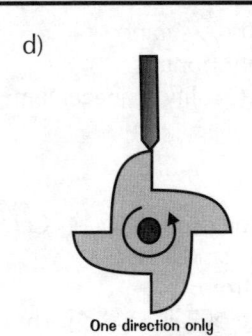

d)

One direction only
Motion: rises and suddenly falls four times every rotation

Q4 The snail cam and the four lobed cam can only work in one direction because there is a sudden jump so the follower would get stuck if the cam was rotated in the wrong direction.

Q5 B, the larger handle, would be easier to turn because it gives you a greater mechanical advantage.

Q6
Slider — Reciprocating motion
Crank — Connecting rod
Rotary motion

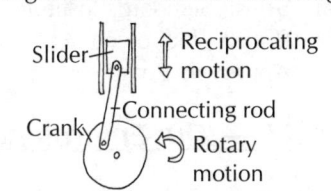

Page 33 — Levers and Links

Q1 Any reasonable examples — e.g.

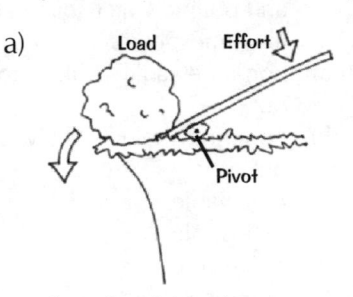

a) Load, Effort, Pivot

In a first class lever the pivot is in between the load and effort. A large load can be lifted with a small effort. The lever gives you a mechanical advantage. This large rock can be lifted by using a smaller rock as a pivot.

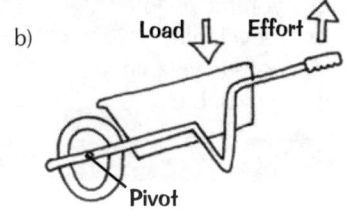

b) Load, Effort, Pivot

In a second class lever the load is in the middle, just like a load in a wheelbarrow

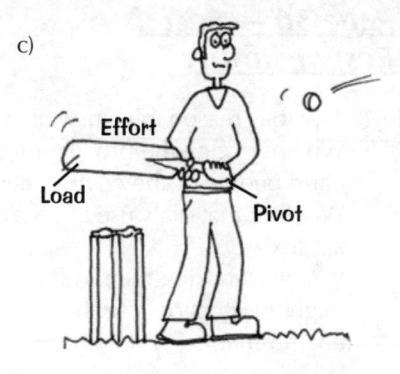

c) Effort, Load, Pivot

A third class lever has the effort in the middle, like when you use a cricket bat. One hand is the pivot point and the other is the effort, while the ball is the load.

Q2
a) a second class lever
b) a third class lever
c) a first class lever
d) a third class lever
e) a first class lever

Q3 The middle wheelbarrow (b) will be the easiest to lift because it has the load closest to the pivot point, giving you the greatest mechanical advantage.

Q4
a) False
b) True
c) False

Q5
a) A link is something that connects different parts of a mechanism together.
b) A link can transfer forces and change the direction of motion.
c) A bell crank changes the direction of a force through 90°.
d) Lazy tongs use loads of levers all linked together.

Section 5 — Market Influences

Page 34 — Product Analysis

Q1 Any 5 from:
• familiarity with manufacturing methods
• understanding the use of different materials
• finding ideas to use in their ideas
• modifying existing designs
• using existing examples to identify good and bad designs
• identifying current styles and fashions

Q2 Accept answers along the lines of:
a) Function is what the product is intended and used for, and how it works.
b) Form is the 'look' of a product — its shape, colour, texture, decoration, etc.
c) Ergonomics is how well the product fits the user / how easy the product is to use.
d) Environmental concerns are things like whether a product has recyclable, reusable or biodegradable parts, whether toxic waste is produced in its manufacture, etc.

Q3 Any 4 sensible answers, e.g.:
• old fashioned look — decorated, moulded, heavy, dark appearance
• modern look — simple, clean, angular, light
• flowing curves
• shape/size
• texture/finish
• colour
• materials... etc.

Q4 Any 8 from:
material — metal or plastic
finish — matt, shiny, leather
colour — silver, black or other
eyepiece or screen
digital or film
type of film — APS, 35mm, polaroid, etc
number of pixels if digital
disposable
cost
ergonomics
provision for a holding strap
zoom facility
tripod attachment

GCSE Resistant Materials Workbook — The Answers

Answers: P.35 — P.38

Q5 Any four from: casting, machining/wasting, fabrication, forging, injection moulding, vacuum forming, extrusion.

Q6 A pre-manufactured part which is fitted into the product as it is being assembled. Examples could be: floppy disc drive in a computer or water pump in a washing machine.

Page 35 — Quality Assurance and Control

Q1 a) standards, meeting
   b) check, meeting
Q2 a) True
   b) False
   c) True
   d) True
   e) False
   f) True
   g) True
   h) False
Q3 micrometer
   It's used to accurately measure and test the dimensional sizes of components.
Q4 Any reasonable sketch e.g. —

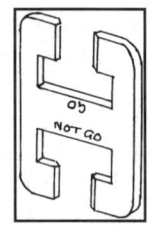

Advantage: Quicker and simpler to use as it needs less skill and no adjustment. Disadvantage: Can only be used for components of the same size as it cannot be adjusted.
Q5 right answer is c)
Q6 a) destructive testing
   b) non-destructive testing

Page 36 — Social Responsibility

Q1 Any four reasonable answers, e.g.
Whether using the product might harm people or the environment.
Whether materials used to make it are toxic.
Whether making the product might harm people or the environment.
Whether recycled, biodegradable or recyclable materials could be used.
Whether workers' conditions are satisfactory.
Whether the product could cause offence to any cultural or religious groups.

Q2 a) user, environment
   b) paint, toxic
   c) emissions, harmful
   d) cultural, religious, offended

Q3 Any two from:
any hand held tool or appliance, any furniture design which must conform to body size — e.g. chairs, tables, desks, beds, sporting equipment such as sledges.

Q4 Any sensible answers, e.g.
back strain, poor circulation in legs, neck strain, increased risk of other muscular strains
Possible modifications include: making the height adjustable so that feet don't need to 'dangle', shaping the back to discourage slouching/support back correctly, adding a neck support, making the back of the chair adjustable or flexible so that you can lean back in it, etc.

Q5 Any reasonable answer, e.g. plastic, paper, glass (not usually wood.)

Page 37 — Consumers

Q1 Without customers there is no need for the product. If no one buys the products then the company will go bankrupt.

Q2 a), e) and f) are all vital

Q3 a) Quality Assurance
   b) Quality Control
   c) Total Quality Management
Q4 1) = b)
   2) = c)
   3) = a)
Q5 It shows the product meets Central European standards.
Q6 Any four from:
The Office of Fair Trading, The British Standards Institution, The Environmental Health Department, The Local Authority Trading Standards Office, The Local Authority Consumer Protection Department, The Citizens' Advice Bureau, The Consumer Advice Council, The National Federation of Consumer Groups, The National Consumer Council.
Q7 a) British Standards Institute
   b) British Electrotechnical Approvals Board

Page 38 — The Environment

Q1 a) The 6,000,000,000,000 people in the world are using the Earth's resources at a frightening rate.
   b) We create too much waste and pollute water sources and the atmosphere.
Q2 a) non-renewable — likely to run out
   b) non-renewable — likely to run out
   c) renewable
   d) renewable
   e) renewable
   f) non-renewable
   g) non-renewable
   h) renewable
   i) renewable
Q3
Q4 a) non-recyclable
   b) recyclable
   c) non-recyclable
   d) recyclable

Answers: P.39 — P.41

Q5 10% (actual amount is 11%)
Q6 about 72%
Q7 Any reasonable answer, e.g. any three from:
Use renewable energy sources — wind, solar, water power.
Use clean energy sources — gas, hydroelectric power.
Have a thermally efficient building — good insulation.
Audit production processes to maximise the use of fuel and eliminate waste.

Page 39 — Health and Safety

Q1 Any reasonable answers, e.g.
a) Wear tough gloves.
b) Wear a leather apron and gloves use tongs when picking it up.
c) Wear a dust mask or make sure the dust extractor is working.
d) Protect your legs with spats, your body with a leather apron and your hands and arms with leather gauntlets. A full face shield would also be needed to protect your head.

Q2 a) Guards must be in place on lathes and drilling machines before starting the machine.
b) Switch off and isolate a machine before carrying out any adjustments.
c) Stop the machine before walking away to do something else.
d) Long hair must be tied back when working to avoid entanglement.
e) Only one person on a machine, at a time, is a very good safety rule to follow.

Q3 A chuck key is used to tighten a drill bit holder. It must be removed before starting machinery, or it could cause damage and injury.

Q4 Any three from: G cramp, vice, sash cramp, jet cramp, mole wrench, bench holdfast, joiners dogs, tongs for hot metal, plus any other appropriate holding device.

Q5 Any reasonable answers e.g.
Risk — sparks (risk of fire), risk of burning himself
Precautions — remove flammable objects from area, wear protective clothing (gauntlets and leather apron), wear eye protection

Page 40 — Health and Safety

Q1 a) A coffee table must be strong enough to stand someone sitting on it without it collapsing.
b) The plastic wheels of a pull-along toy must be securely fastened to the axles so that they cannot be pulled off and become a choking hazard.
c) A metal desk lamp must be electrically earthed so that the user is not electrocuted.

Q2 Any three from:
disc brakes, power brakes, anti-lock brakes, crumple zones, air bags, collapsible steering wheel, smooth soft surfaces in the cabin, seat belts, seat belt pre-tensioners

Q3 Any reasonable answers, e.g.
Securely fastened eyes.
Hard-wearing fabric which doesn't shed fluff (a possible choking hazard).
No loose parts to pull off (e.g. ears).
Strong construction so stuffing does not come out.

Q4 Any reasonable answers, e.g.
Strong construction, so it doesn't collapse.
Hand rail to provide stability for the user.
Platform to stand at top or put bucket/paint on.
No sharp edges.
Light construction for carrying — aluminium would be a suitable material.
Non-slip treads.

Q5 a) no responsibility
b) approve designs
c) prosecute suppliers
d) no responsibility
e) approve electrical appliances

Section 6 — Industrial Awareness

Page 41 — Scale of Production

Q1
Jobbing Production:
Making a single, one-off product
Made to meet the customer's individual and specific requirements.
Labour intensive, and requires a highly skilled workforce.
Examples include one-off buildings e.g. The Millennium Dome.

Batch Production:
Making a specific quantity of a product
Batches can be repeated as many times as required.
The machinery and labour used need to be flexible.
Down time is unproductive and needs to be kept to a minimum.

Mass Production:
Making products on a really large scale.
You need a large, unskilled workforce.
Different stages are broken down in to simple repetitive tasks.
The specialised equipment required is very expensive.

Continuous Production
Non-stop production 24hrs/day.
The specialised equipment required is very expensive.
Examples include oil and chemical manufacture.

Q2 It will come under jobbing production, because it is a single one-off product, made to a set of individual and specific requirements.

Q3 Any reasonable answer, e.g. Yes, generally the more you produce of something, the cheaper it will become. For example, a car handmade by a highly skilled workforce, like Rolls Royce, will be expensive. A mass-produced car, quickly made in a factory by robots, will be a lot cheaper.

GCSE Resistant Materials Workbook — The Answers

Answers: P.42 — P.45

Page 42 — Manufacturing Systems

Q1 a) Cell production is where the manufacture of a product is <u>split</u> in to individual components, each made by a different <u>team</u> of people, called a <u>cell</u>.
b) Within each cell the team is <u>responsible</u> for all aspects of the production of their <u>component</u>, including <u>quality</u> control and <u>maintenance</u> of the machines.
c) The main advantages of this method include <u>teamwork</u>, good <u>communication</u> and high quality of the finished product.

Q2 Most of the production line is automated. Unskilled labour is used mainly for simple assembly tasks, with a small number of semi-skilled operators. This ensures there's a continuous flow along the production line.

Q3 Flexible Manufacturing Systems. The key to its success is to have flexible workforce and machinery which are able to do a variety of jobs.

Q4 Just in Time. You only buy materials and components as and when you need them, in order to save time, space and money.

Page 43 — CAD / CAM and CIM in Industry

Q1 Computer-Aided Design — it means using computers to design things.

Q2 Computer-Aided Manufacture — manufacturing using computer controlled machines. It refers to any part of the design process that's controlled by a computer system.

Q3 Linking CAD and CAM together involves the use of specialised computer software that converts data from drawings into machining instructions.

Q4 a) CIM is the system by which different <u>stages</u> of the <u>design process</u> are <u>linked</u> together by a central <u>computer system</u>.
b) CIM helps to <u>coordinate</u> different stages in the design process, and the central computer system makes <u>communication</u> easy.
c) The really clever bit is the <u>software</u>, that will automatically <u>update</u> any changes made and will alert all related stages. This can save a lot of <u>time</u> and eliminate costly <u>mistakes</u>.

Q5 a) CAD — Computer-Aided Design = point 3
b) CAM — Computer-Aided Manufacture = point 5
c) CAD/CAM — Computer-Aided Design and Manufacture = point 1
d) CIM — Computer Integrated Manufacture = point 4
e) CNC — Computer Numerical Control = point 2

Page 44 — Advertising and Marketing

Q1 a) 3   b) 1   c) 5
d) 2   e) 4

Q2 The British Standards Institution is a quality control organisation that sets out standards, testing procedures, and quality assurance techniques.

Q3 A Kitemark proves that a product meets the BSI standards, and has undergone rigorous tests, for example on safety and quality.

Q4 ISO 9000 is an international standard of quality that gets awarded to companies that have good quality assurance.

Q5 Any five reasonable answers, e.g. newspapers, magazines, mail, television, radio, cinema, posters, e-mail, Internet, on the back of a bus

Q6 Market research enables you to find out who your customers are and what their needs are.

Q7 <u>Things to include</u>:
brief questions
inoffensive questions
multiple choice questions
tick boxes
questions where the answers are easy to use and analyse
relevant and clear questions
<u>Things to Avoid</u>:
long questions
too many questions
irrelevant information
open ended questions

Page 45 — Good Working Practice

Q1 Any reasonable answer — e.g. A flow chart is a simple diagram showing the order that things happen in.

Q2 a) <u>A sausage shape</u> is used for the start and finish of a flow chart.
b) <u>A rectangle</u> is used to show a process or action.
c) <u>A diamond</u> is used for decisions or questions.
d) <u>An arrow</u> is used to link any of the stages together.

Q3
```
      START
        ↓
FILL KETTLE WITH
WATER + TURN ON
        ↓
PUT INSTANT COFFEE
    INTO MUG
        ↓
 ADD BOILING
    WATER
        ↓
   ADD MILK
        ↓
ADD SUGAR, STIR  ←┐
  AND TASTE       │
        ↓         │
    IS IT      NO │
 SWEET ENOUGH?────┘
        ↓ YES
     FINISH
```

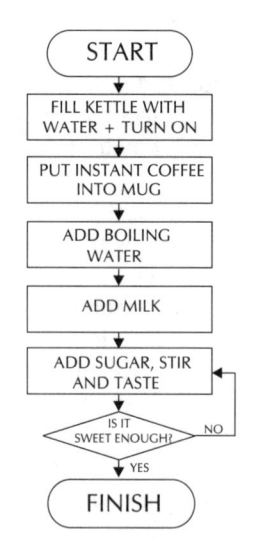

Answers: P.46

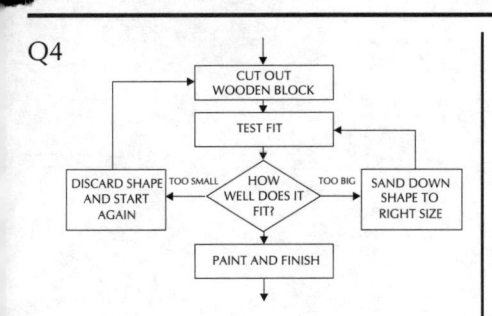

Q4

```
       ↓
  CUT OUT
  WOODEN BLOCK
       ↓
   TEST FIT  ←──────────────┐
       ↓                    │
DISCARD SHAPE ← TOO SMALL   │ TOO BIG → SAND DOWN
AND START      HOW WELL            SHAPE TO
AGAIN          DOES IT FIT?        RIGHT SIZE
       ↓
  PAINT AND FINISH
       ↓
```

Page 46 — Jigs, Moulds and Templates

Q1 A template is normally a shape that you draw round, in order to reproduce any number of identical shapes. It must be hardwearing so that it can be used repetitively without wearing down.

Q2 a) A simple strip of metal with holes accurately drilled in it could be used as a drilling jig. You need to clamp the jig to the wood and then simply drill through the existing holes.

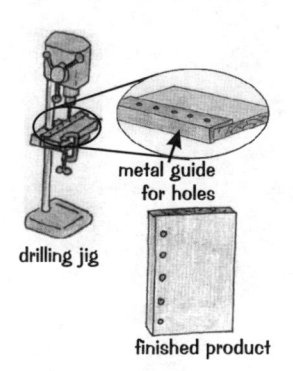

(drilling jig — metal guide for holes — finished product)

b) 1. It will speed up the production process.
2. It will help improve accuracy, making every component identical.

Q3 a) <u>Moulds</u> are commonly used in <u>plastics</u> manufacturing, in processes like <u>vacuum forming</u>.

b) Once an <u>accurate</u> mould has been made, detailed plastics shapes can be formed with it <u>over and over</u> again.

c) Industrial moulds are <u>expensive</u> to produce, so a manufacturer needs to be <u>certain</u> of their design, and needs to be able to make <u>large</u> numbers of their product to make it cost-effective.

Q4 a) False
b) True
c) True
d) True
e) False